D0175017

To:

_____

From:

_____

365 devotions to inspire your day

hug's™

Daily
Inspirations for
Women

HOWARD BOOKS
A DIVISION OF SIMON & SCHUSTER
New York   London   Toronto   Sydney

Our purpose at Howard Books is to:

- *Increase faith* in the hearts of growing Christians
- *Inspire holiness* in the lives of believers
- *Instill hope* in the hearts of struggling people everywhere

Because He's coming again!

Published by Howard Books, a division of Simon & Schuster
1230 Avenue of the Americas, New York, NY 10020

Hugs Daily Inspirations for Women © 2006 by Freeman-Smith LLC

Library of Congress Cataloging-in-Publication Data
Hugs daily inspirations for women : 365 devotions to inspire your day.
    p. cm
    1. Christian women—Prayer-books and devotions—English. 2. Devotional calendars. I. Howard Publishing Co.
BV4844.H785 2005
242'.643—dc22

2005052531

ISBN-13: 978-1-4165-3388-7
ISBN-10:   1-4165-3388-5

30 29 28 27 26 25 24 23 22 21

HOWARD and colophon are registered trademarks of Simon & Schuster, Inc.

Manufactured in China

For information regarding special discounts for bulk purchases, please contact Simon & Schuster Special Sales at 1-800-456-6798 or business@simonandschuster.com.

Written by Criswell Freeman
Edited by Between the Lines
Interior design by Bart Dawson
Cover design by Stephanie D. Walker

We never know how high we are
till we are called to rise.
And then, if we are true to plan,
our statures touch the skies.

—Emily Dickinson

Introduction

You deserve a hug today—lots of hugs! And so, for that matter, do your family and friends. These hugs can take several forms: the physical hugs may range from a slight pat on the back to a full-strength bear hug. But other "hugs," while more subtle, can be just as effective.

You can share an emotional hug when you offer a kind word to a friend or family member. You can share a spiritual hug when you offer a quiet prayer for a person in need. You can share a hug of faith when you offer a word of encouragement to someone who is discouraged or fearful or both. In short, you can share feelings of love and affection through your words, through your actions, and through your prayers.

This book contains 365 inspirational readings that are intended to help you prepare your mind for the opportunities to give—and to receive—as many hugs as possible throughout the day. This text is also intended to make you smile and to make you think. It contains Bible verses, quotations, and brief essays—all of which can help lift your spirits and shape your day.

Every day (including this one) provides opportunities to give hugs and to receive them—opportunities to share smiles, to offer kind words, and to perform small acts of kindness that can make a big difference in the lives of those you love. So without further delay, let the hugs begin!

January

Hugs of Encouragement

*Let's see how inventive we can be
in encouraging love and helping out.*
Hebrews 10:24 MSG

How many people will you hug today? How many times will you share a smile, a kind word, or a pat on the back? How many times today will you demonstrate—by your words and your actions—that you are a caring woman?

When you feel happy and secure, you may find it easy to share kind words and heartfelt hugs. But when you're discouraged or tired, it may seem difficult to encourage anyone (including yourself).

Anna Quindlen correctly observed, "Love is not leisure, it is work." So even on those days when the dog bites or the bee stings, you should be quick to do the "work" required to give—and receive—love. After all, the world still needs all the hugs it can get . . . especially yours.

*Love is a fruit in season
and within reach of every hand.*
Mother Teresa

Faith or Fear?

*The LORD keeps watch over you as you
come and go, both now and forever.*
Psalm 121:8 NLT

As a busy woman, you know from experience that life is not always easy or fair. But even when you don't understand why the world unfolds as it does, never lose faith in God's ability through you to make a difference in that little corner of the world you call home.

Helen Keller advised, "Faith is a spiritual spotlight that illuminates the path." Her words remind us that faith can—and should—be the hallmark of a well-lived life.

So the next time you find yourself facing a fear-provoking situation, ask yourself which is stronger: your faith or your fear. The answer should be obvious. Whatever your challenge, whatever your question, whatever mountain you must climb, God is there, and He will help you work things out. Your job is to keep the faith until He does.

*God will never let you sink under
your circumstances. He always provides
a safety net, and His love always encircles.*
Barbara Johnson

Excitement Is Contagious

Do your work with enthusiasm.
Work as if you were serving the Lord,
not as if you were serving only men and women.
Ephesians 6:7 NCV

The year was 1963, and she was in her mid-forties. She took her life savings, started her own business, and began selling cosmetics the hard way—door to door, one customer at a time. The business grew because of her ability to enlist the enthusiastic support of an energetic sales force. Today that business still ranks among the leaders in the cosmetics industry.

Her name? Mary Kay Ash. Her advice? "A mediocre idea that generates enthusiasm will go further than a great idea that inspires no one." So the next time opportunity knocks on your door, open it with enthusiasm. Excitement is contagious. But if you want to change the world, the first person you must inspire is yourself.

A person's mind is not a container to be filled,
but rather a fire to be kindled.
Dorothea Brande

The Wisdom to Be Grateful

Do everything without complaining or arguing.
Then you will be innocent and without any wrong.
Philippians 2:14–15 NCV

Mary Cassatt has been honored on a U.S. postage stamp; her works are found in the world's finest art galleries; and she was the noted pupil of the great Edgar Degas. But her most enduring legacy may be the role she played in introducing French Impressionist art to America.

Cassatt, a woman making it in a field that was at the time considered men's work, didn't complain. In fact, she said, "It would be ungracious to grumble." And, she might have added, unproductive.

So if you find yourself regularly attending gripe sessions or pity parties, ask yourself this question: What am I not doing to improve my situation? Then it's time to cease all self-pity and get busy. After all, on the canvas of life it's never too late to paint a beautiful picture.

Live today fully, expressing gratitude for all you have
been, all you are right now, and all you are becoming.
Melody Beattie

Trust for the Future

> *"I say this because I know what I am planning*
> *for you," says the LORD. "I have good plans for you, not*
> *plans to hurt you. I will give you hope*
> *and a good future."*
> Jeremiah 29:11 NCV

Life is like a garden. Each day God gives us opportunities to plant seeds for the future. When we plant wisely—and when we face the future with trust, optimism, hope, and determination—the harvest is bountiful.

Are you willing to place your future in God's hands? And are you willing to do your part to help your family, your friends, and yourself? Hopefully so, because you have the power to change the world— the power to improve the lives of your loved ones, your friends, and your neighbors.

God created you for a very important reason: His reason. You have much important work to do—and the best time to begin that work is now.

> *Never be afraid to trust*
> *an unknown future to a known God.*
> Corrie ten Boom

Relationships That Matter

How wonderful, how beautiful,
when brothers and sisters get along!
Psalm 133:1 MSG

As we travel along life's road, we exchange countless hugs and build lifelong relationships with a small, dear circle of family and friends. And how best do we build and maintain these relationships? Healthy relationships are built upon honesty, compassion, responsible behavior, trust, and optimism. Healthy relationships are built upon the Golden Rule. Healthy relationships are built upon sharing and caring.

Are you the kind of woman who spends the time and the energy required to build strong, healthy, lasting relationships? Barbara Bush had this advice: "Cherish your human connections—your relationships with friends and family." And that's wise counsel because you are blessed, you are loved, and you are vitally important to your family and friends—they most certainly need you, and you most certainly need them.

Line by line, moment by moment, special times are
etched into our memories in the permanent ink
of everlasting love in our relationships.
Gloria Gaither

Beyond Worry

*Give all your worries and cares to God,
for he cares about what happens to you.*
1 Peter 5:7 NLT

Because life is sometimes difficult, and because we have understandable fears about the uncertainty of the future, we worry. At times we may find ourselves fretting over the countless details of everyday life. We may worry about our relationships, our finances, our health, or any number of potential problems—some large and some small.

If you're a worrier by nature, it's probably time to reconsider the way you think. Perhaps you've formed the unfortunate habit of focusing too intently on negative aspects of life and spending too little time counting your blessings. If so, take your worries to God—and leave them there. When you do, you'll learn to worry a little less and to trust God a little more—and that's as it should be, because God is trustworthy, you are protected, and your future can be intensely bright.

A ruffled mind makes a restless pillow.
Charlotte Brontë

Sparkle!

Observe people who are good at their work—
skilled workers are always in demand and admired.
Proverbs 22:29 MSG

Born in 1928, she became the biggest box-office draw in America by the tender age of ten. Amazingly, millions of fans still love to watch her childhood performances. What's the attraction of movies made so long ago? The films seem as fresh today as they did then, in part because of the advice a mother gave young Shirley Temple. Just before the director shouted, "Action," Shirley's mom whispered one word in her daughter's ear: "Sparkle." It was little Shirley's reminder to concentrate and give the performance her full attention.

All of us can benefit from the one-word cue that helped make Shirley Temple a star. So whether you're at work, home, school, or play, remember today and every day to sparkle. Your audience will love you for it.

I pray, but I don't pray to win.
I pray for the inspiration to give my best.
Althea Gibson

The Wisdom to Laugh

There is a time to cry and a time to laugh.
There is a time to be sad and a time to dance.
Ecclesiastes 3:4 NCV

Laughter is a special gift from God, a gift He intends for us to use. Yet sometimes, because of the inevitable stresses of everyday living, we fail to find the fun in life. When we allow life's inevitable disappointments to cast a pall over our lives and our souls, we do a profound disservice to ourselves and to our loved ones.

If you've allowed the clouds of life to obscure the blessings of life, perhaps you've formed the unfortunate habit of taking things just a little too seriously. If so, it's time to fret less and laugh more.

Today, look for the humor that surrounds you—when you do, you'll find it. And remember: God created laughter for a reason, and Father indeed knows best. So laugh!

If you could choose one characteristic that would get you through life, choose a sense of humor.
Jennifer Jones

Your Attitude of Gratitude

Be cheerful no matter what; pray all the time;
thank God no matter what happens.
1 Thessalonians 5:16–18 MSG

For most of us, life is busy and complicated. We have countless responsibilities, some of which begin before sunrise and many of which end long after sunset. Amid the rush and crush of the daily grind, it is easy to lose sight of our blessings. But when we forget to slow down and say thank you for the gifts we've been given, we rob ourselves of opportunities to thank God for all the blessings we have received.

We can either rush through the day with scarcely a word of thanksgiving, or we can slow down and give thanks. Kahlil Gibran said, "Wake at dawn with a winged heart and give thanks for another day of loving." When we follow that advice, gratitude becomes its own reward . . . but not its only reward.

A sense of gratitude will help open our eyes
to the things God has done in the past
and the things He will do in the future.
Emilie Barnes

A Hug for Yourself:
The Wisdom to Be an Optimist

*My cup runs over. Surely goodness and mercy shall
follow me all the days of my life; and I will dwell
in the house of the LORD forever.*
Psalm 23:5–6 NKJV

Audrey Meadows was an optimist by nature and
by training. Audrey was born in China, where
her parents served as missionaries. She later returned
to America, began an acting career in New York, and
eventually won the part of Alice Kramden on the
old TV classic *The Honeymooners*. Miss Meadows's
advice for life was straightforward: she said, "It was
my mother's belief and mine to resist any negative
thinking." The rest of us should take note.

Optimism is a gift you give to yourself—a way of
putting self-fulfilling prophecy to work for you. So
if you find yourself focusing on your fears instead of
on your faith, it's time for an Audrey Meadows–style
attitude adjustment. It's time to trust yourself, your
future, and your God.

*One of the things I learned the hard way was
that it doesn't pay to get discouraged.
Keeping busy and making optimism
a way of life can restore your faith in yourself.*
Lucille Ball

The Power of Words

*Be gracious in your speech. The goal is to
bring out the best in others in a conversation,
not put them down, not cut them out.*
Colossians 4:6 MSG

Our attitudes are contagious. If we're optimistic and upbeat, we'll spread optimism wherever we go. But if we fall prey to pessimism and doubt, our friends and loved ones will suffer right along with us.

Are you fully aware of the power of your words? The words you speak—and the tone in which those words are spoken—have the power to lift others up or to bring them down.

You have the power to be a source of encouragement to your loved ones—and they need that kind of encouragement. So remember the words of Lydia Maria Child, the author and social reformer who said, "An effort made for the happiness of others lifts us above ourselves." And then start lifting!

*The battle of the tongue is won
not in the mouth, but in the heart.*
Annie Chapman

Proud to Be Here

You have made known to me the path of life;
you will fill me with joy in your presence.
Psalm 16:11 NIV

The woman they called the "Queen of Country Comedy" was actually a college graduate and the daughter of a prominent businessman. She was Sarah Colley (when she married she became Sarah Cannon), but the world knew her best as the character she created: Minnie Pearl.

Minnie always began her act with the same phrase: "Howdeeeee! I'm just so proud to be here." And those words should apply to each of us as we step onto the stage of life.

Today, in honor of the Southern socialite who became the grand matron of the Grand Old Opry, celebrate a grand and glorious life—yours. When you do, your star will shine, just like Miss Minnie's.

One filled with joy preaches without preaching.
Mother Teresa

Embracing Change

*There is a time for everything, and
a season for every activity under heaven.*
Ecclesiastes 3:1 NIV

Anne Morrow Lindbergh gained fame as the
bride of aviator Charles Lindbergh, and her
1955 book, *Gift from the Sea*, was a bestseller. Anne
had sound advice about the changing tides of life: "It
is only in growth, reform, and change, paradoxically
enough, that true security is found."

For each of us, real security means mastering the
art of sailing our little boats on the shifting seas of
life. Sometimes life's waters are smooth; sometimes
they're choppy.

When you encounter changing conditions, as
you most certainly will from time to time, be flexible,
be persistent, and be optimistic. When you learn to
embrace change—when you learn to go and to grow
with the flow, it's clear sailing ahead.

*With God, it isn't who you were that matters;
it's who you are becoming.*
Liz Curtis Higgs

Sailing through the Storms of Life

Jesus answered, "Why are you afraid? You have so little faith!" Then he stood up and rebuked the wind and waves, and suddenly all was calm.

Matthew 8:26 NLT

Sometimes the seas of life are calm, and sometimes they are not. When we find ourselves beset by the inevitable storms of life, we may sense that all is lost—but if we imagine, even for a moment, that all hope is gone, we are mistaken.

The Bible is not ambiguous: it promises that God will remain steadfast, even during our darkest hours. God's Word makes it clear that He is with us always, on good days and bad days. He never leaves our side, and He never stops loving us.

So if you're feeling buffeted by the winds and the waves of life, don't despair. God has promised to protect you now and forever. And upon that promise, you can always depend.

Like the winds of the sea are the ways of fate as we voyage through our life. 'Tis the set of the soul that decides the goal and not the storm or the strife.

Ella Wheeler Wilcox

The Way We Look at Our Friends

Jacob said, "For what a relief it is to see your friendly smile. It is like seeing the smile of God!"
Genesis 33:10 NLT

Jennie Jerome, a vivacious New York socialite, had definite ideas about friendship and about love. While on vacation in Europe, Jennie met a young British nobleman, Lord Randolph Churchill. It was love at first sight, and three days later Lord Randolph proposed. The couple was married, and they had a son—a very notable son named Winston Churchill, the man who led Great Britain through the dark days of World War II.

Jennie Jerome Churchill, a New Yorker with a decidedly English perspective, had this advice for building friendships. She said, "Treat your friends as you do your pictures, and place them in their best light." That's great advice no matter what side of the Atlantic you happen to call home.

In her heart of hearts, a woman draws her emotional strength, and sometimes even her physical energy, from her relationships.
Dianna Booher

Do It with Feeling

You make me glad by your deeds, O Lord;
I sing for joy at the works of your hands.
Psalm 92:4 NIV

Virginia Patterson Hensley was a country singer whose talent was so big that she seemed destined to become a star. She performed under her married name, Cline, and became a country music legend—the incomparable Patsy Cline.

Patsy Cline's advice for success on stage was as simple and straightforward as her music. She said, "If you can't do it with feeling, don't." That advice applies to all of us, whether or not we can carry a tune in the proverbial bucket.

You're on stage every day of your life, whether at work, at home, or at school. And when you perform with enthusiasm, that enthusiasm is contagious. You have the power to give the world a performance worth remembering. And when you "do it with feeling," your audience will surely agree that the feeling is mutual.

Each day, look for a kernel of excitement.
Barbara Jordan

Contentment That Lasts

*We brought nothing into this world, and it is certain
we can carry nothing out. And having food and
raiment let us be therewith content.*
1 Timothy 6:7–8 KJV

Everywhere we turn, or so it seems, the world promises us contentment and happiness. The world's messages tell us we'll be content if we look a certain way, if we behave in a certain fashion, and if we accumulate a certain number of material possessions. But the contentment the world offers is fleeting and incomplete. Thankfully, genuine contentment—the contentment that results in a lasting sense of inner peace—is not found in shopping malls.

Happiness depends less on our possessions than on our thoughts. When we focus on our blessings instead of on our shortcomings, we make our lives richer. You have the power to obtain that joy. So claim the contentment and joy that can—and should—be yours.

Peace within makes beauty without.
Old Saying

On Those Difficult Days

*The LORD is my rock and my fortress and my deliverer;
the God of my strength, in whom I will trust.*

2 Samuel 22:2–3 NKJV

All of us face those occasional days when traffic backs up and the dog gobbles up the homework. But when we find ourselves overtaken by the minor frustrations of life, we must catch ourselves, take a deep breath, and lift our thoughts upward.

Although we must occasionally struggle to rise above the distractions and disappointments of everyday living, we never need to struggle alone. God is here—eternally and faithfully, with infinite patience and love. And our friends and family members can help restore perspective and peace to our souls.

The Russian-born writer Ayn Rand had this advice for dealing with tough times: "Face a challenge and find joy in the capacity to meet it." With God's help, and with the help of family members and friends, you can meet your challenges—and you will!

*When life is difficult, God wants us
to have a faith that trusts and waits.*

Kay Arthur

Hope and Happiness

But happy are those . . .
whose hope is in the LORD their God.
Psalm 146:5 NLT

Hope and happiness are traveling companions. After all, God is good, His love endures, and we have every reason to be hopeful. But sometimes in life's darker moments, we may lose sight of these blessings, and when we do, it's easy to lose hope. Yet if we sincerely desire to lead happier, healthier lives, we will learn to live by faith.

Are you a hope-filled woman? You should be. You have an array of talents within you and an assortment of opportunities before you. You have the potential to achieve your goals and the wherewithal to accomplish your dreams. So remember the words of Maya Angelou, who observed, "The horizon leans forward, offering you space to place new steps of change." Step toward your horizon with assurance and hope. It's the happy—and healthy—way to live.

The greater part of our happiness or misery depends
on our dispositions, and not our circumstances.
Martha Washington

Staying the Course

*Even though good people may be bothered
by trouble seven times, they are never defeated.*
Proverbs 24:16 NCV

When Althea Gibson was born in South Carolina, the odds against her winning a Wimbledon championship were about a billion to one. But apparently no one told her. In an era when African-Americans weren't even allowed to play on most tennis courts, Gibson fashioned herself into a champion. She practiced whenever she could, and when Althea was finally allowed to play, she was ready. She won the French Open, the U.S. Open, and Wimbledon.

Althea Gibson's life reminds us that failure is always the path of least persistence. So if you're facing long odds, remember the story of a young girl, without a court to play on, who didn't know she couldn't do it . . . so she did. And so, for that matter, can you.

*Just don't give up trying to do what you really
want to do. Where there's love and inspiration,
I don't think you can go wrong.*
Ella Fitzgerald

Trusting His Guidance

*Every morning he wakes me. He teaches me to listen
like a student. The Lord G*OD* helps me learn.*
Isaiah 50:4–5 NCV

God promises to guide us if we will let Him. Our job, of course, is to let Him. But sometimes we'll be tempted to do otherwise. Sometimes we'll be tempted to go along with the crowd; other times we'll be tempted to do things our way, not God's way. When we feel those temptations, we need to resist them.

We need to ask ourselves what we will allow to guide us through the coming day: our own desires (or the desires of our friends)? Or will we allow God to lead the way? The answer should be obvious. We should let God be our guide. When we entrust the future to Him, God gives us the strength to meet any challenge and the courage to face any trial.

*Walk in the daylight of God's will because then
you will be safe; you will not stumble.*
Anne Graham Lotz

Comforting Others

*He comforts us in all our affliction, so that we may be
able to comfort those who are in any kind of affliction,
through the comfort we ourselves receive from God.*
2 Corinthians 1:4 HCSB

The world can be a difficult and dangerous place,
a place where our friends and family members
often face challenges that test their courage and
dampen their spirits.

But each day provides countless opportunities to
encourage our loved ones, to assist the needy, and
to comfort the brokenhearted. When we do these
things, we spread seeds of hope and happiness—and
that's precisely what we should do.

Today, when you encounter someone who needs
a helping hand or a comforting word, be generous
with both. You possess the power to make the world
a better place one person—and one hug—at a time.
When you use that power wisely, you make your own
corner of the world a kinder, gentler, happier place.

*A woman softens her own troubles by
generously solacing those of others.*
Françoise d'Aubigné Maintenon

Take Your Best Shot

*You know that under pressure, your faith-life is
forced into the open and shows its true colors.
So don't try to get out of anything prematurely.
Let it do its work so you become mature and
well-developed, not deficient in any way.*
James 1:3–4 MSG

Geena Davis is a legitimate Hollywood star, with
an Oscar on the mantel to prove it. But at age
forty, she decided to take up the sport of archery.
She approached the bow and arrow with the same
intensity she brought to her movie roles, and after
two years of practice Geena had become one of the
best archers in America. Her secret is simple. She
says, "I don't worry about the results. My goal is to
do my best and to have fun."

If you have a habit of putting too much pressure
on yourself, remember Geena's advice and lighten
up. Work hard, but don't fret over results—just clear
your mind and take your best shot. Then, like Ms.
Davis, you'll have a better chance of hitting the
bull's-eye.

*Give the world the best you have,
and the best will come back to you.*
Madeline Bridges

Giving Hugs, Accepting Hugs

Let love and faithfulness never leave you . . .
write them on the tablet of your heart.
Proverbs 3:3 NIV

When is the best time to give a hug to a friend or family member? Whenever you can. And when is the best time to ask for a hug? Whenever you feel you need one.

Hugs—genuine and heartfelt—are a physical demonstration of the love we feel for others. That's why we should be quick to give hugs and just as quick to receive them.

Mother Teresa once said, "Kind words can be short and easy to speak, but their echoes are truly endless." The same can be said for hugs. So do yourself and your loved ones a world-class favor: hug with abandon—because you and your loved ones need every single hug you can get.

A hug is the ideal gift . . . one size fits all.
Author Unknown

Relax!

Relax, everything's going to be all right;
rest, everything's coming together;
open your hearts, love is on the way!
Jude 1:2 MSG

She grew up in the tiny town of Winchester, Tennessee, yet in the course of her career, Dinah Shore earned ten Emmy awards, recorded seventy-five hit records, and hosted a string of hit TV shows. Obviously, Dinah was a hard worker. But she was also a woman who took time to relax. And so should you.

Ms. Shore's philosophy was simple: she said, "Play is a vital part of life." Dinah believed that hard work should be punctuated by rest and relaxation, and she was right. So if you're overworked, overcommitted, or underinspired, give yourself a much-needed break. You deserve time to rest, to relax, and to recharge your batteries. Do yourself and the world a favor: carve out the time you need to restore your energy, your optimism, your perspective, and your faith.

Each day, and the living of it, has to be a conscious
creation in which discipline and order are relieved
with some play and pure foolishness.
May Sarton

Love Is a Choice

Beloved, if God so loved us,
we ought also to love one another.
1 John 4:11 KJV

Love is a choice. Either we choose to behave lovingly toward others . . . or not; either we conduct ourselves in ways that enhance our relationships . . . or not. But we should be aware that genuine love requires effort. Simply put, if we wish to build lasting relationships, we must be willing to do our part.

Building lasting relationships requires compassion, wisdom, empathy, kindness, courtesy, and forgiveness (lots of forgiveness). If that sounds like work, it is—which is perfectly OK, since the rewards of love always outweigh the costs.

Zora Neale Hurston observed, "Love makes your soul crawl out of its hiding place." You are capable of choosing that kind of love—and the world becomes a better place when you do.

Nobody has ever measured, not even poets,
how much the heart can hold.
Zelda Fitzgerald

Good Thinking

*Set your mind on things above,
not on things on the earth.*
Colossians 3:2 NKJV

Because we are human, we're always busy with our thoughts. We simply can't help ourselves. Our brains never shut off—even while we're sleeping, we mull things over. The question is not if we will think; the question is how we will think and what we will think about.

The American poet Phoebe Cary observed, "All the great blessings of my life are present in my thoughts today." Her words can apply to you.

You will make your life better when you focus on your blessings, not your misfortunes. So do yourself and your loved ones a favor: learn to think optimistically about the world you live in and the life you lead. Then prepare yourself for the blessings good thoughts will bring.

*Believe that your tender, loving thoughts and
wishes for good have the power to help
the struggling souls of the earth rise higher.*
Ella Wheeler Wilcox

Purposeful Living

> GOD *made everything with a place and purpose.*
> *Proverbs 16:4 MSG*

Life is best lived on purpose, not by accident—the sooner we discover what God intends for us to do with our lives, the better. But the search to find meaning and purpose is seldom easy. Sometimes we wander aimlessly in a wilderness of our own making. And sometimes we must try—and fail—many times before we discover our life's work.

Mother Teresa said, "We are all pencils in the hand of God." And author Willa Cather noted, "This is happiness: to be dissolved in something complete and great." How true.

Today is a wonderful day to dissolve yourself in something important. You can do it—and if you get busy, you will.

> *There is wonderful freedom and joy in coming*
> *to recognize that the fun is in the becoming.*
> *Gloria Gaither*

Critics Beware

*Let's agree to use all our energy in getting along
with each other. Help others with encouraging words;
don't drag them down by finding fault.*
Romans 14:19–20 MSG

From experience we know that it's easier to criticize than to correct. We know it's easier to find faults than solutions. Yet the urge to criticize others remains a powerful temptation for most of us.

Negativity is highly contagious: we give it to others, who, in turn, give it back to us. This cycle can be broken by positive thoughts, sincere prayers, encouraging words, and heartfelt hugs.

As thoughtful women seeking to build better lives for ourselves and a better world for our neighbors, we should seek to be encouragers, not critics. When we do, God smiles . . . and so do our families and friends.

*If I long to improve my brother, the first step
toward doing so is to improve myself.*
Christina Rossetti

The Power of Enthusiasm

Whatever you do, work at it with all your heart,
as working for the Lord, not for men.
Colossians 3:23 NIV

Singer Ethel Merman was best known for her show-stopping performance in *There's No Business Like Show Business.* She was one of Broadway's brightest stars, headlining such classics as *Gypsy* and *Anything Goes.* Her face was even featured on a U.S. postage stamp.

Ms. Merman said, "Always give your audience the old fire, even when you feel like a cake of ice." That's great advice no matter what "stage" you're on. Because at work, home, or school, you'll discover that your audience can't really get excited about your performance until you do.

You have an important message to share with the world, so share it with enthusiasm. The world needs your enthusiasm, and you'll be blessed with rewards when you share your gifts enthusiastically and often.

Everything worthwhile—everything of any lasting
value—is the result of effort and enthusiasm.
Loretta Young

February

Relationships Built upon Honesty

*Tell each other the truth
because we all belong to each other.*
Ephesians 4:25 ICB

Honesty is the best policy, but it is not always the easiest policy. Sometimes the truth hurts, and sometimes it's tough to be a woman of integrity. Tough, but essential.

Author Catherine Marshall correctly observed, "The single most important element in any human relationship is honesty—with oneself, with God, and with others." Wise women agree.

Integrity is built slowly over a lifetime. It's the sum of every right decision and every honest word. It is forged on the anvil of honorable work and polished by the twin virtues of honesty and fairness. Integrity is a precious thing—difficult to build but easy to tear down. We must make certain that we weave integrity into the fabric of our lives, beginning now and ending never.

The most exhausting thing in life is being insincere.
Anne Morrow Lindbergh

When Storm Clouds Form

> *Let us run with endurance*
> *the race that is set before us.*
> Hebrews 12:1 NASB

When the sun is shining and all is well, it's easy to have faith. But when life takes an unexpected turn for the worse, as it will from time to time, your faith will be tested. In times of trouble and doubt, God remains faithful to you—and you must retain faith in yourself.

Social activist Jane Addams commented, "You do not know what life means when all the difficulties are removed. It's like eating a sweet dessert the first thing in the morning." And so it is with your own life.

The next time you spot storm clouds on the horizon, remind yourself that every difficult day must come to an end—and when tough times are tough, tough women (like you) are tougher.

I want faith—not that everything will go as I want,
but that God will be there and that this will be enough.
Sheila Walsh

Too Busy to Hug?

Don't burn out; keep yourselves fueled and aflame.
Romans 12:11 MSG

Sometimes, when our to-do lists are filled to overflowing, we feel as though there isn't a minute to spare. But we should never be too busy to share an encouraging word or a heartfelt hug with our family members and friends.

Saint Teresa of Avila believed, "The nicest thing we can do for our heavenly Father is to be kind to one of His children." And Barbara Johnson noted, "Sometimes one little spark of kindness is all it takes to reignite the light of hope in a heart that's blinded by pain." These words serve as timely reminders that we should never be too busy to spread kindness as we pass through this world. And the best moment to share a kind hug or a gentle word is this one.

Getting things accomplished isn't nearly
as important as taking time for love.
Janette Oke

Keeping Possessions in Perspective

> *A pretentious, showy life is an empty life;*
> *a plain and simple life is a full life.*
> Proverbs 13:7 MSG

We live in an era of prosperity, a time when many of us have been richly blessed with an assortment of material possessions that our forebears scarcely could have imagined. Because we live in such prosperous times, we must be cautious to keep prosperity in perspective.

The world often stresses the importance of material possessions, but we should not. Corrie ten Boom reflected, "I have held many things in my hands, and I have lost them all; but whatever I have placed in God's hands, that I still possess." And Mary Morrison Suggs warned, "We are made spiritually lethargic by a steady diet of materialism." These words remind us that in the grand scope of a well-lived life—a well-lived life like yours—material possessions aren't nearly as important as some people might want you to think.

> *Keeping up with the Joneses is like keeping up*
> *with a scared jackrabbit—only harder.*
> Marie T. Freeman

Respect

Show respect for all people.
Love the brothers and sisters of God's family.
1 Peter 2:17 ICB

Shari Lewis entertained and educated countless children with puppet creations named Lamb Chop, Hush Puppy, and Charlie Horse. She and her daughter, Mallory, became the first mother-daughter team ever to win a joint Emmy Award. Shari's advice for raising respectful children was simple. She said, "What you give, you get. If you give real respect to your child, then respect becomes a family habit."

Even if you're tired or frustrated or both, remember to spread around as much respect as you can—starting at home. It's the right thing to do. Besides, as Shari was quick to point out, you get what you give in this old world. So why not give while the getting is good?

It is our calling to treat every human being with
grace and dignity, to treat every person,
whether encountered in a palace or a gas station,
as a life made in the image of God.
Sheila Walsh

A Foundation of Faith

The fundamental fact of existence is that this trust in God, this faith, is the firm foundation under everything that makes life worth living.
Hebrews 11:1 MSG

When Mary McLeod Bethune was born to former slaves in 1875, few would have guessed that she would one day change the face of American education. But she did. After teaching school for only five years, she founded the Daytona Normal and Industrial Institute for Negro Girls. Today that Florida school is known as Bethune-Cookman College.

In the beginning Mary McLeod Bethune operated on a shoestring—she had almost no resources . . . except her faith. Bethune once observed, "Without faith nothing is possible. With it, nothing is impossible." So the next time you come face to face with the illusion of impossibility, remember that faith is the foundation upon which great schools—and great miracles—are built. It's up to you to believe—and to achieve—accordingly.

I never really look for things.
I accept whatever God throws my way.
Whichever way God turns my feet, I go.
Pearl Bailey

Embracing a Life of Prayer

Be joyful in hope, patient in affliction,
faithful in prayer.
Romans 12:12 NIV

Is prayer an integral part of your daily life, or is it a hit-and-miss occasional activity? Do you "pray without ceasing," or is your prayer life an afterthought? As you consider the role prayer currently plays in your life—and the role you think it should play—remember that the quality of your spiritual life is inevitably related to the quality of your prayer life.

Prayer changes things, and it changes you. So today, instead of turning things over in your mind, turn them over to God in prayer. Instead of worrying about your next decision, pray about it. Don't limit your prayers to meals or to bedtime. Pray often about things great and small. God is listening, and He wants to hear from you. Now.

Prayer begins where human capacity ends.
Marian Anderson

Generosity Now

It is more blessed to give than to receive.
Acts 20:35 ICB

Two years after her husband died, Joan Kroc founded the Ronald McDonald House Charities and became its largest benefactor. Once, when she read a newspaper headline about flooding in South Dakota, she sent unsolicited donations to flood victims totaling fifteen million dollars. This generous woman was the widow of Ray Kroc, the founding father of McDonald's restaurants.

Joan's philosophy was simple. She looked for people in need, and then she surprised them with her generosity. You can do the same. Whatever your financial situation, you can make a big difference in the lives of others. And every time you do, you'll discover, as Joan did, how good it feels to share the wealth.

I must admit that I personally measure success in terms of the contributions an individual makes to her or his fellow human beings.
Margaret Mead

New Beginnings, New Celebrations

*Do not remember the former things, nor consider
the things of old. Behold, I will do a new thing.*
Isaiah 43:18–19 NKJV

Each new day offers countless opportunities to celebrate life and to serve others. But each day also offers countless opportunities to fall prey to the many distractions of our difficult times.

Consider this day a new beginning. Consider it a fresh start, a renewed opportunity to serve your friends and family with willing hands and a loving heart.

Gigi Graham Tchividjian, daughter of evangelist Billy Graham, spoke for women everywhere when she observed, "How much of our lives are, well, so daily. How often our hours are filled with the mundane, seemingly unimportant things that have to be done, whether at home or work. These very 'daily' tasks could—and should—become a celebration."

Make your life a celebration. After all, your talents are unique, as are your opportunities. So the best time to really live—and really celebrate—is now.

*What a wonderful life I've had!
I only wish I'd realized it sooner.*
Sidonie Gabrielle Colette

Perseverance Pays

Indeed we count them blessed who endure.
James 5:11 NKJV

Amid the glitz of Hollywood, Katherine Hepburn's tastes tended toward men's shirts and khaki pants. Nominated for an incredible twelve Academy Awards, she won four times. But this cinematic legend was not overly impressed with her own talents or, for that matter, the talents of others. She said, "Genius is simply the infinite capacity for taking life by the scruff of the neck."

If you'd like to make your star shine a little more brightly, don't worry about your intellect; worry about your persistence. Genius doesn't guarantee success, but persistence pays. When you face tough times, remember Katherine Hepburn and take life fearlessly by the scruff of the neck. Because the greatest genius of all is sometimes nothing more than the genius it takes to persevere.

There is no chance, no destiny,
no fate, that can hinder or control
the firm resolve of a determined soul.
Ella Wheeler Wilcox

The Kinds of Habits to Make (or Break)

*Do not be deceived: "Evil company
corrupts good habits."*
1 Corinthians 15:33 NKJV

It's an old saying and a true one: first you make your habits, and then your habits make you. Some habits (the healthy kind) improve the quality of your life, while other habits (the unhealthy variety) inevitably hurt you and your loved ones.

The Roman poet Ovid said, "Nothing is stronger than habit." And the Roman poet Henri Frédéric Amiel advised, "To learn new habits is everything, for it is to reach the substance of life. Life is but a tissue of habits." So here's a word to the wise: if you want to improve your life, improve your habits.

You have the power to form healthier habits. You have the power to improve your life. You have the power to create a new, healthier you. Exercise that power by taking control of your life today.

*If you want to form a new habit, work hard.
If you want to break a bad habit, work harder.*
Marie T. Freeman

The Quality of Your Handiwork

But as for you, be strong and do not give up,
for your work will be rewarded.
2 Chronicles 15:7 NIV

Lucille Ball's TV show ranked number one for four short years, but it has remained wildly popular for more than four decades. Why? For one thing, she and her husband, Desi Arnaz, were the first producers to put their shows on film.

In the early days of television, shows were recorded on poor-quality gadgets called kinescopes. For modern audiences such recordings are almost unwatchable. Film was more expensive, but Lucy and Desi used it, and millions of people are glad they did.

The next time you've got a big job, don't cut corners. It may cost a little more to make something that lasts, but go for it. Who knows? The world may be admiring your handiwork long after you're gone. Make it something worth looking at!

Quality is a proud and soaring thing.
Jessica Julian

Hugs for Those in Need

Be generous: Invest in acts of charity.
Charity yields high returns.
Ecclesiastes 11:1 MSG

Born in El Paso, Texas, in 1902, Irene Ryan went on to enjoy a fine career in Vaudeville and on radio. But she didn't become a household name until she landed the role of Granny on the 1960s TV sitcom *The Beverly Hillbillies*. In 1971, two years before her death, Irene donated a million dollars to endow a foundation that has provided scholarships to worthy students for more than three decades, and it's still going strong.

Irene Ryan may be best remembered as a wiry TV grandma, but her greatest legacy is the countless lives she's touched—which just goes to show that whether you're a Beverly Hillbilly, a TV star, or just plain folks real charity can last a lifetime . . . and beyond.

These are three things that God especially loves:
true faith with a pure heart, a simple life
with a religious spirit, and openhandedness
inspired by charity.
Ita of Killeedy

February 14

Above and Beyond the Daily Grind

Careful planning puts you ahead in the long run;
hurry and scurry puts you further behind.
Proverbs 21:5 MSG

Because you're a citizen of the twenty-first century, you're probably busy . . . very busy. But here's a question: are you able to squeeze time into your hectic schedule for the things that matter most—things like family, friends, rest, exercise, and worship? Hopefully so. But if you're having trouble putting first things first—or if you find yourself putting them off altogether, it's time to reshuffle your priorities.

You live in a noisy world, a world filled with distractions, frustrations, temptations, and complications. But if you allow the commotion of everyday life to distract you from your most important priorities, you'll be doing yourself and your loved ones a disservice. Don't make that mistake. Instead, put first things first and let lesser things take care of themselves.

One cannot manage too many affairs—
like pumpkins in the water, one pops up
while you're trying to hold the others down.
Chinese proverb

Self-Made?

*Humble yourselves therefore under the mighty hand
of God, that he may exalt you in due time.*
1 Peter 5:6 KJV

When you experience success, it's easy to look squarely into the mirror and proclaim, "I did that!" But it's wrong. Pride—especially when it is exaggerated or misplace—can lead to disaster.

The English writer Emily Brontë observed, "Proud people breed sad sorrows for themselves." And her words still ring true. Excessive amounts of pride can lead to trouble, and lots of it.

In truth, there is no such thing as a self-made man or woman. All of us are made by God and helped by a long list of family and friends, people who have lightened our loads and guided our steps. And if we're wise, we will happily share the credit.

*What makes humility so desirable is the marvelous thing
it does to us; it creates in us a capacity for
the closest possible intimacy with God.*
Monica Baldwin

Keeping Life in Focus

*Steep your life in God-reality, God-initiative,
God-provisions. Don't worry about missing out.
You'll find all your everyday
human concerns will be met.*
Matthew 6:33 MSG

What is your focus today? Are you willing to center your thoughts on the countless blessings God has bestowed on you? Before you answer that question, consider this: the direction of your thoughts will determine, to a surprising extent, the direction of your day and your life.

This day—and every day hereafter—is a chance to celebrate the life God has given you. It's a chance to celebrate your relationships, your talents, and your opportunities. So focus on the gift of life and on the blessings that surround you.

You're a beautiful creation of God, a being of tremendous worth and importance. Give thanks for your gifts and share them. Never have the needs—or the opportunities for service—been greater.

Life isn't a matter of milestones but of moments.
Rose Kennedy

Celebrating Others

> *Do not withhold good from those who deserve it.*
> Proverbs 3:27 NLT

Do you delight in the victories of others? You should. Each day offers opportunities to encourage others and to praise their good works. When you do so, you spread seeds of joy and happiness.

American poet Ella Wheeler Wilcox advised, "Talk happiness. The world is sad enough without your woe." Her words ring true. Yet all too often, we allow ourselves to become so overwhelmed by the demands of daily life that we forget to "talk happiness" to our family members and friends.

Life is a team sport, and all of us need occasional pats on the back from our teammates. So be cheerful, with a smile on your face and encouraging words on your lips. By blessing others, you'll also bless yourself. And when you do, God smiles.

> *As you're rushing through life, take time to stop*
> *a moment, look into people's eyes, say something kind,*
> *and try to make them smile!*
> Barbara Johnson

Anything's Possible!

The things which are impossible
with men are possible with God.
Luke 18:27 NKJV

Face facts: we live in a miraculous universe. Our presence bears testimony to God's miraculous power to create something from nothing. But the miracles don't stop there. God is not limited to big bangs or biblical events. He continues to craft wonders all around us: the miracle of the birth of a new baby; the miracle of a world renewing itself with every sunrise; the miracle of a life transformed or a body healed.

Each day God's handiwork is evident for all to see and experience. His miracles come in a variety of shapes and sizes, so keep your eyes and your heart open. Be watchful, and you'll soon be amazed.

I could go through this day oblivious to the miracles
all around me, or I could tune in and "enjoy."
Gloria Gaither

When You Need Rest

I said to myself, "Relax and rest.
GOD has showered you with blessings."
Psalm 116:7 MSG

Even the most energetic women will, from time to time, find themselves running on empty. You will too. The inevitable demands of daily life can drain you of your strength and rob you of the joy that can and should be yours. When you're feeling tired, discouraged, or worse, pay attention—it's time to get some rest.

Ovid offered this advice: "Take a rest; a field that has rested gives a bountiful crop." Whether you're a farmer or a city slicker, that's a tip worth taking.

Are your physical or spiritual batteries running low? Is your energy on the wane? Are your emotions frayed? If so, it's time to turn your thoughts and your prayers to God. And when you're finished, it's probably time to turn off the lights and go to bed!

Taking care of yourself physically really helps
emotionally. People who get a lot of sleep,
who do the things that relieve stress,
can withstand a lot of stress.
Laura Bush

Pity Parties R Not Us

Patient endurance is what you need now,
so you will continue to do God's will.
Then you will receive all that he has promised.
Hebrews 10:36 NLT

Wilma was the twentieth of twenty-two children. As a child she contracted polio and wore a brace to help her walk. But amazingly, just five years after taking that brace off her left leg, this determined sprinter won a bronze medal in the 1956 Olympics. Four years later, in Rome, Wilma Rudolph became the first woman to win three gold medals in a single Olympic competition.

If you're ever tempted to feel sorry for yourself (and who isn't?), remember a little girl who was stricken with polio—a little girl who grew up to become a world-champion sprinter. And remember that the race of life is indeed a marathon—one in which those who persevere are usually the ones who grab the gold.

We can do anything we want to do
if we stick to it long enough.
Helen Keller

Count Your Many Blessings

I will bless them and the places surrounding my hill.
I will send down showers in season;
there will be showers of blessing.
Ezekiel 34:26 NIV

Most of us have been blessed beyond measure, but sometimes, as busy people living in a demanding world, we're slow to count our gifts and even slower to give thanks to the Giver. Our blessings include life and health, family and friends, freedom and possessions—for starters. And those blessings are multiplied when we share them with others.

As the old saying goes, "When we drink the water, we should remember the spring." So it's appropriate that those of us who have been richly blessed should give thanks for our gifts, no matter how busy we are.

Do you make it a habit to slow down each day and thank God for your talents, your opportunities, and your loved ones? If so, you've already learned that gratitude is its own reward—but not its only reward.

The art of thanksgiving is thanksliving.
Author Unknown

Pleasing God

So we make it our goal to please him.
2 Corinthians 5:9 NIV

In a scene from the movie *Chariots of Fire*, a Scottish missionary named Eric Liddell explained why he was preparing to run in the 1924 Olympics. Liddell said that God had made him for a purpose: to be a missionary in China. But he added that God had also given him the ability to run fast. Liddell concluded by saying, "When I run, I feel God's pleasure."

God created you with a unique set of talents and opportunities. When you use those talents to the fullest, then you, like Eric, may sense God's pleasure.

Marie Curie observed, "Life is not easy for any of us. But what of that? We must have perseverance and above all confidence in ourselves. We must believe that we are gifted for something and that this thing must be attained." And her words apply to you!

Make God's will the focus of your life day by day.
If you seek to please Him,
you'll find yourself satisfied with life.
Kay Arthur

Making It Happen

> *"I say this because I know what I am planning*
> *for you," says the LORD. "I have good plans*
> *for you, not plans to hurt you.*
> *I will give you hope and a good future."*
> Jeremiah 29:11 NCV

She graduated with honors from one of the best law schools in the country but received few job offers. Why? Because in 1952 many people thought women weren't supposed to be lawyers. Three decades later, after a distinguished career and with remarkably little animosity about past slights, Sandra Day O'Connor became the first female justice of the United States Supreme Court.

If you feel that you've suffered unfair treatment, remember Justice O'Connor. Invest your energy in making things better today, not in rehashing the past. The trials in life are difficult enough without bitterness and regret. Besides, when it comes to your future, the jury is still out, and the verdict is up to you. You can't afford to dwell on yesterday—you've got to get on the case today. You can do it, and if you don't give up, you will.

Life's ups and downs provide windows of opportunity
to determine your values and goals. Think of using all
obstacles as steppingstones to build the life you want.
Marsha Sinetar

February 24

*Accepting Forgiveness . . .
and Giving It*

*Smart people know how to hold their tongue;
their grandeur is to forgive and forget.*
Proverbs 19:11 MSG

God's power to forgive, like His love, is infinite.
All who are the recipients of God's forgiveness
should forgive others. When we do, we not only
obey God's command, we also free ourselves from
a prison of our own making; a prison of bitterness
and regret.

Jennie Jerome Churchill noted, "Life is not
always what one wants it to be, but to make the best
of it, as it is, is the only way of being happy." These
words remind us that when we allow ourselves to
become embittered, we forfeit the happiness that
might otherwise be ours.

When it comes to forgiveness, God doesn't
play favorites, and neither should we. Complete
forgiveness is God's way, and it should be our way
too. Anything less is an affront to Him and a burden
to us.

*Nobody is perfect.
Look for the good in others.
Forget the rest.*
Barbara Bush

Growing Up

When I was a child, I spoke as a child,
I understood as a child, I thought as a child;
but when I became a man, I put away childish things.
1 Corinthians 13:11 NKJV

God doesn't intend for any of us to be stagnant. Far from it! God's plan for us includes a lifetime of personal and spiritual growth—a lifetime of learning from our experiences and sharing what we've learned.

We can and should continue to grow throughout every stage of life. If we cease to grow, either emotionally or spiritually, we do ourselves and our loved ones a profound disservice.

It's a familiar saying, and it's true: "You aren't getting older, you're getting better!" And it's up to you to keep getting better every day you live. When you do, you'll continue to shine your light on a world that needs all the maturity and wisdom it can get.

Only in growth, reform, and change,
paradoxically enough, is true security to be found.
Anne Morrow Lindbergh

February 26

Passion and Purpose

*Never be lazy in your work,
but serve the Lord enthusiastically.*
Romans 12:11 NLT

We all need to discover a purpose for our lives, a purpose that excites us and causes us to live each day with passion.

Anna Quindlen had this advice: "Consider the lilies of the field. Look at the fuzz on a baby's ear. Read in the backyard with the sun on your face. Learn to be happy. And think of life as a terminal illness, because, if you do, you will live it with joy and passion, as it ought to be lived."

If you have not yet discovered a passionate pursuit that blesses you and your world, don't be discouraged. Keep searching and keep trusting that with God's help, you can—and will—find a meaningful way to serve your neighbors, your Creator, and yourself.

*Whatever you choose to do, you have one other
obligation, and that is to yourself. Do it with passion.
If you've not yet found your passion, keep searching.
You never know when it will find you.*
Condoleezza Rice

The Importance of Friends

God gave us this command:
Those who love God must also
love their brothers and sisters.
1 John 4:21 NCV

In 1950 an Associated Press poll voted Babe Didrikson Zaharias the outstanding female athlete of the first half of the twentieth century. And she earned it. Babe was the 1932 Olympic gold medalist in both the javelin and the eighty-meter hurdles. But she didn't stop there.

After her career in track and field was completed, Babe took up the sport of golf and fashioned herself into one of the best women golfers in history. Looking back on her life, though, Babe observed, "Winning has meant much to me, but winning friends has meant even more." Her words remind us that few things in life are more important than the enduring bonds of friendship. Let us never forget that lesson, and let us never forget our friends.

Friends are like a quilt with lots of different shapes,
sizes, colors, and patterns of fabric. But the end result
brings you warmth and comfort in a support system
that makes your life richer and fuller.
Suzanne Dale Ezell

The Time for Action

The kingdom of God is present not in talk but in power.
1 Corinthians 4:20 NCV

Abigail Adams was married to founding father and second U.S. president John Adams for fifty-four years. When her son John Quincy Adams was also elected to that office, she became the first woman to be both the wife and the mother of U.S. presidents. This amazing mom warned, "We have too many high sounding words, and too few actions that correspond with them." Her wisdom reminds us of the need to do the right thing—and to do it sooner rather than later.

If you'd like to jumpstart your career or your life, try Abigail's formula for success: use a little less talk and a little more action. Because it doesn't take a president's wife or mother to realize that millions of good intentions pale in comparison to a single good deed.

When people made up their minds that they wanted
to be free and took action, there was a change.
Rosa Parks

March

What Doesn't Change

*Change your hearts and lives because
the kingdom of heaven is near.*
Matthew 3:2 NCV

We live in a world that is always changing, but we worship a God who never changes—thank goodness! That means we can be comforted in the knowledge that our heavenly Father is the rock that simply cannot be moved: "I am the LORD, I do not change" (Malachi 3:6 NKJV).

The next time you face unwelcome changes, remember that some things never change—things like the love you feel in your heart for your family and friends . . . and the love God feels for you. So instead of worrying too much about life's inevitable challenges, focus your energies on finding solutions. Have faith in God's ability to work through you, do your best to solve your problems, and leave the rest up to God.

*Let nothing disturb you, nothing frighten you;
all things are passing; God never changes.*
Saint Teresa of Avila

Embraced by God

Give thanks to the LORD, for he is good;
his love endures forever.
Psalm 118:29 NIV

Every day of our lives—indeed, every moment of our lives—we are embraced by God. He's always with us, and His love for us is deeper and more profound than we can imagine.

Songwriter and speaker Gloria Gaither once observed, "Being loved by Him whose opinion matters most gives us the security to risk loving too—even loving ourselves."

Actress and author Lisa Whelchel gives this advice: "Believing that you are loved will set you free to be who God created you to be. So rest in His love and just be yourself."

Let these words serve as a powerful reminder: you are a marvelous, glorious being, created by a loving God who wants you to become—completely and without reservation—the woman He created you to be.

Snuggle in God's arms. When you are hurting,
when you feel lonely or left out, let Him
cradle you, comfort you, and reassure you.
Kay Arthur

Laughter Keeps You Young!

A cheerful disposition is good for your health;
gloom and doom leave you bone-tired.
Proverbs 17:22 MSG

Would you like a proven formula for maintaining a youthful countenance? Here it is: laugh as often as you can. It's a simple, yet effective, formula for a happier, healthier life.

Few sounds on earth can equal the happy reverberations of friends laughing together. Few joys in life can compare with a good laugh and a good friend to share it with. And it's also worth noting that God has given each of us the gift of laughter for a very good reason: to use it.

Hearty laughter is food for the soul and medicine for the heart. So do yourself this favor: acquire the habit of looking at the humorous side of life. When you do, you'll discover that, whatever your age, a good laugh can make you just a little bit younger.

Laughter is the language of the young at heart
and the antidote to what ails us.
Barbara Johnson

Mixed Messages

We live by faith, not by sight.
2 Corinthians 5:7 NIV

Sometimes it's hard being a woman of faith, especially when the world keeps pumping out messages that are contrary to your beliefs.

Beware! The media is working around the clock in an attempt to rearrange your priorities. The media often conveys that appearance is central and that social standing is all-important. But guess what? Those messages are untrue. The important things in life have little to do with appearances. The truly important things in life have to do with your faith, your family, and your future.

Living in the twenty-first century, you are relentlessly bombarded by media messages that are contrary to your faith. Take those messages with a grain of salt—or better yet, don't take them at all.

There can be no happiness if the things
we believe in are different from the things we do.
Freya Stark

Improving Your Corner of the World

Whoever wants to become great among you must serve the rest of you like a servant.
Matthew 20:26 NCV

You are a wondrous creation treasured by God—how will you respond? Will you consider each day a glorious opportunity to celebrate life and improve your little corner of the world? Hopefully so, because your corner of the world, like so many others, can use all the help it can get.

Former Miss America Nicole Johnson observed, "We only live once, and if we do it well, once is enough." You can make a difference—a big difference—in the quality of your own life and the lives of your neighbors, your family, and your friends.

You make the world a better place whenever you find a need and fill it. And in these difficult days, the needs are great—but so are your abilities to meet them.

I am only one, but still I am one;
I cannot do everything, but still I can do something;
I will not refuse to do the something I can do.
Helen Keller

Relying on the Creator

*He gives power to the weak, and to those
who have no might He increases strength.*
Isaiah 40:29 NKJV

Have you ever faced challenges that seemed too
big to handle? Big problems that, despite your
best efforts, simply could not be solved? If so, you
know how uncomfortable it is to feel helpless in the
face of difficult circumstances. Thankfully, you can
always turn your thoughts and prayers to God and
He will respond.

God's hand uplifts those who turn their hearts
and prayers to Him. Count yourself among that
number. When you do, you can live courageously
and joyfully, knowing that "this too will pass"—
but that God's love for you will not. And you can
draw strength from the knowledge that you are a
marvelous creation, loved, protected, and uplifted
by the ever-present hand of God.

*So rejoice! You are giving Him what
He asks you to give Him—the chance
to show you what He can do.*
Amy Carmichael

Beyond the Darkness

Why are you cast down, O my soul?
And why are you disquieted within me?
Hope in God; for I shall yet praise Him,
the help of my countenance and my God.
Psalm 42:11 NKJV

Grief visits all of us who live long and love deeply. When we lose a loved one, or when we experience any other profound loss, darkness overwhelms us for a while. We feel as though we cannot summon the strength to face another day— but with God's help, we can.

God promises that He is "close to the broken-hearted" (Psalm 34:18 NIV). In times of intense sadness, we can turn to Him, and we can turn to close friends and family. When we do, we can be comforted . . . and in time we will be healed.

Concentration-camp survivor Corrie ten Boom said, "There is no pit so deep that God's love is not deeper still." Let us remember those words and live by them . . . especially when the days seem dark.

God is good, and heaven is forever.
These two facts should brighten up
even the darkest day.
Marie T. Freeman

Sharing Words of Hope

A good person's words will help many others.
Proverbs 10:21 ICB

One way we can give "emotional hugs" to our loved ones is by sharing words of encouragement and hope. Hope, like other human emotions, is contagious. In fact, hope is highly contagious—as is its opposite.

When we associate with hope-filled friends and family members, we are encouraged by their faith and optimism. But if we spend too much time in the company of naysayers and pessimists, our attitudes, like theirs, tend to become cynical and negative.

Today look for reasons to celebrate God's endless blessings. And while you're at it, look for people who will join you in the celebration. You'll be better for their company, and they'll be better for yours.

Don't forget that a single sentence, spoken at the right moment, can change somebody's whole perspective on life. A little encouragement can go a long, long way.
Marie T. Freeman

The Wisdom of Acceptance

He is GOD. Let him do whatever he thinks best.
1 Samuel 3:18 MSG

Sometimes we must accept life on its terms, not our own. Life has a way of unfolding not as we will, but as it will. And sometimes there is precious little we can do to change things.

When events transpire that are beyond our control, we have a choice: we can either learn the art of acceptance, or we can make ourselves miserable as we struggle to change the unchangeable.

We must entrust the things we cannot change to God. Once we have done so, we can prayerfully and faithfully tackle the important work He has placed before us: doing something about the things we can change . . . and doing it now.

I pray hard, work hard, and leave the rest to God.
Florence Griffith Joyner

To Judge or Not to Judge

Judge not, and ye shall not be judged:
condemn not, and ye shall not be condemned:
forgive, and ye shall be forgiven.
Luke 6:37 KJV

From time to time all of us fall prey to a powerful yet subtle temptation: the temptation to judge others. But the Bible teaches us to refrain from such behavior. The warning is unmistakably clear: "Judge not, and ye shall not be judged." In other words, we must refrain from being judgmental . . . or else.

Thankfully, the Bible promises that God has forgiven us (whew!). Now it's our turn to forgive others. So let's refrain from the temptation to judge our family members, our friends, and our loved ones. And let's refrain from judging people we don't know very well (or people we don't know at all). Instead, let's forgive everybody (including ourselves) in the same way God forgives: completely.

Perhaps the greatest blessing that
religious inheritance can bestow is an open mind,
one that can listen without judging.
Kathleen Norris

Dealing with Difficult People

Real wisdom, God's wisdom, begins with a holy life
and is characterized by getting along with others.
It is gentle and reasonable, overflowing with mercy.
James 3:17 MSG

Face it: sometimes people can be difficult. When they are, we may be tempted to strike back, either verbally or in some other way. But usually there's a better way—and our job is to find it.

Best-selling author Susan L. Taylor correctly observed, "Not everybody is healthy enough to have a front-row seat in your life." In other words, the best way to deal with some difficult people is to distance yourself from them.

As long as you live here on earth, you'll face countless opportunities to lose your temper when other folks behave badly. But God has a better plan: He wants you to forgive and move on.

When something robs you of your peace of mind,
ask yourself if it is worth the energy you are
expending on it. If not, then put it out of
your mind in an act of discipline. Every time
the thought of "it" returns, refuse it.
Kay Arthur

Give Me Patience, Lord . . . Now!

Knowing God leads to self-control.
Self-control leads to patient endurance,
and patient endurance leads to godliness.
2 Peter 1:6 NLT

A re you a woman in a hurry? If so, you may be in for a few disappointments. Why? Because life has a way of unfolding according to its own timetable, not yours. That's why life requires patience—and lots of it!

Lamentations 3:25 reminds us that "the LORD is wonderfully good to those who wait for him and seek him" (NLT). But for most of us, waiting quietly is difficult because we're in such a hurry for things to happen.

The next time you find your patience tested to the limit, slow down, take a deep breath, and relax. Sometimes life can't be hurried—and during those times patience is indeed a priceless virtue.

The key to everything is patience.
You get the chicken by hatching the egg,
not by smashing it.
Ellen Glasgow

Maintaining Perspective

It's important to look at things from God's point of view.
1 Corinthians 4:6 MSG

If a temporary loss of perspective has left you worried, exhausted, or both, it's time to readjust your thought patterns. Negative thoughts are habit forming; thankfully so are positive ones. With practice you can form the habit of focusing on God's priorities and your own possibilities. When you do, you'll soon discover that you spend less time fretting about your challenges and more time solving them.

Elisabeth Kübler-Ross observed, "It's only when we truly know and understand that we have a limited time on earth—and that we have no way of knowing when our time is up—that we will begin to live each day to the fullest, as if it were the only one we had."

That's perspective. And that's life. May you have heaping helpings of both.

The proper perspective creates within us a spirit of reaching outside of ourselves with joy and enthusiasm.
Luci Swindoll

Our Children, Our Treasures

*I have no greater joy than to hear that
my children walk in truth.*
3 John 4 KJV

Each child is different, but every child is similar in this respect: he or she is a priceless gift from God. And with the Father's gift comes immense responsibility.

Our children are, without question, our most precious resource. As responsible adults we must create homes in which the future generation can grow and flourish.

Today let us pray for our children—all of them. Pray for children here at home and for children around the world. Every child is God's child. May we, as concerned adults, summon the wisdom, the courage, and the strength to protect those precious little ones who cannot protect themselves.

*Children are not so different from kites.
Children were created to fly. But they need wind,
the undergirding and strength that comes from
unconditional love, encouragement, and prayer.*
Gigi Graham Tchividjian

His Rightful Place

Step out of the traffic! Take a long, loving look at me,
your High God, above politics, above everything.
Psalm 46:10 MSG

A s we think about the nature of our relationship
with God, we remember this: we will always have
some type of relationship with Him—it is inevitable
that our lives must be lived in relationship to God.
The question is not if we will have a relationship
with Him; the burning question is whether that
relationship will be one that seeks to honor Him.

Have you spent much time lately thinking about
your own relationship with God? Or have you been
too busy to invest a few moments each day in quiet
reflection? When you pause each morning to count
your blessings and consult your Creator, you'll find
perspective and strength for the day ahead.

Thankfully, God is always available, He's always
ready to forgive, and He's waiting to hear from you
now. The rest, of course, is up to you.

God has put into each of our lives a void that
cannot be filled by the world. We may leave God
or put Him on hold, but He is always there,
patiently waiting for us . . . to turn back to Him.
Emilie Barnes

Character, Character, Character

*Applying all diligence, in your faith
supply moral excellence.*
2 Peter 1:5 NASB

Wise women understand that integrity is a crucial building block in the foundation of a well-lived life. Character is a precious thing—difficult to build, but easy to tear down. Thoughtful women like you value it and protect it at all costs.

Living a life of integrity isn't always the easiest way, but it is always the right way. If we find ourselves tempted to break the truth—or even to bend it—we must remember that character and wisdom are traveling companions.

Actress Jacqueline Bisset believed that beauty is related to character too. She said, "Character contributes to beauty. It fortifies a woman as her youth fades. A mode of conduct, a standard of courage, discipline, fortitude and integrity can do a great deal to make a woman beautiful." When you're a woman of character, you're always beautiful.

Character building begins in infancy and ends in death.
Eleanor Roosevelt

The Search for Contentment

*Keep your lives free from the love of money and be
content with what you have, because God has said,
"Never will I leave you; never will I forsake you."*
Hebrews 13:5 NIV

Where can you find contentment? Is it a result of
wealth, power, beauty, or fame? Hardly. Genuine
contentment springs from a thankful heart.

Our modern world seems preoccupied with
the search for happiness. We're bombarded with
messages telling us that happiness depends upon
the acquisition of material possessions. But these
messages are false. Contentment is not the result
of acquiring *more* but of being thankful for what we
already have.

Thus, contentment is really a choice we
make—a choice to be *thankful*. Contentment is not
as elusive as it may seem; it is yours for the *thanking*.
Lift your thanks to the Creator of all that's good,
and as you thank Him for the blessings in your
life—and in the lives of others—you will find your
contentment grow.

*If I could just hang in there, being faithful to
my own tasks, God would make me joyful and content.
The responsibility is mine, but the power is His.*
Peg Rankin

Doing the Right Thing Right Now

> *In everything set them an example
> by doing what is good.*
> Titus 2:7 NIV

Hers was not a typical childhood. She grew up half a world away, the daughter of missionaries. And she called upon her childhood experiences to write a series of novels about the Chinese people. A Nobel Prize winner, her masterpiece was *The Good Earth.*

She, of course, was Pearl Buck, and she said, "You cannot make yourself feel something you do not feel, but you can make yourself do right in spite of your feelings."

It's easy to do something when you feel like doing it—emotions can be powerful motivators. It's considerably harder to do something for no other reason than the simple fact that you know it's the right thing to do. But remember: it's always the right time to do what's right. Always.

> *If we do the wrong thing, we are quite likely
> never to know what we have lost by it.*
> Laura Ingalls Wilder

Celebrating with a Hug and a Smile

Celebrate God all day, every day. I mean, revel in him!
Philippians 4:4 MSG

Life should never be taken for granted. Each day is a priceless gift from God and should be treated as such.

Author Hannah Whitall Smith observed, "How changed our lives would be if we could only fly through the days on wings of surrender and trust!" And Clement of Alexandria said, "All our life is a celebration for us; we are convinced, in fact, that God is always everywhere. We sing while we work . . . we pray while we carry out all life's other occupations." These words remind us that this day is God's creation, a gift to be treasured and savored.

Today let us celebrate life with smiles, with kind words, and with hugs. After all, this is God's day, and we are commanded to rejoice and be glad. So let the celebration begin!

Today is mine. Tomorrow is none of my business.
If I peer anxiously into the fog of the future,
I will strain my spiritual eyes so that I will
not see clearly what is required of me now.
Elisabeth Elliot

Courage for Today

Be strong and courageous, and do the work.
Do not be afraid or discouraged,
for the LORD God, my God, is with you.
1 Chronicles 28:20 NIV

Amelia Earhart was the first woman to fly solo across the Atlantic. That made her one of the most notable figures of the first half of the twentieth century. But she remains best known for what we don't know about her. While attempting to fly around the world in 1937, Amelia's plane vanished in the Pacific. No trace was ever found.

Amelia once said, "Courage is the price life extracts for peace." She understood that all too often we're held back by irrational fears that cause us to put life on hold.

Of course, you should never take foolhardy risks. But if you're looking for a surefire way to give yourself a boost, look life squarely in the eye and do the courageous thing.

It's the peaceful way to live.

Courage is the ladder on which all other virtues mount.
Clare Boothe Luce

God's Power to Renew

Those who wait on the LORD shall renew their strength;
they shall mount up with wings like eagles, they shall
run and not be weary, they shall walk and not faint.
Isaiah 40:31 NKJV

For busy women living in a fast-paced, twenty-first-century world, life may seem like a merry-go-round that never stops spinning. If that description seems to fit your life, you may find yourself running short of patience or strength—or both.

When you feel tired or discouraged, there is a source from which you can draw the power needed to recharge your spiritual batteries. That source is God.

Are you exhausted or troubled? Weak or worried? Worn down or burned out? If so, have a heart-to-heart talk with God. When you do, you'll discover that the Creator of the universe can help you gain a renewed sense of hope and a fresh perspective. Your job is to let Him do it.

Birds sing after the storm. Why shouldn't we?
Rose Kennedy

Our Greatest Refuge

*It is better to take refuge in the LORD
than to trust in man.*
Psalm 118:8 HCSB

God is our greatest refuge. When every earthly support system fails, God remains steadfast, and His love remains unchanged. When we encounter life's inevitable disappointments and setbacks, God remains faithful. When we suffer losses that leave us breathless, God is always with us, always ready to respond to our prayers, always working in us and through us to turn tragedy into triumph.

Author and speaker Patsy Clairmont observed, "If you are walking toward Jesus to the best of your ability, he will see you through life's unpredictable waters—but you must risk launching the boat." And that's sound advice, because even during life's most difficult days, God stands by us. Our job, of course, is to return the favor and stand by Him.

*Whether our fear is absolutely realistic
or out of proportion in our minds,
our greatest refuge is Jesus Christ.*
Luci Swindoll

Beyond Guilt

> *People are happy if they can do
> what they think is right without feeling guilty.*
> Romans 14:22 NCV

All of us have made mistakes. Sometimes our failures result from our own shortsightedness. On other occasions we're swept up in events that are beyond our control. Under either set of circumstances, we may experience feelings of guilt. But God has an answer for the guilt we feel. That answer is His forgiveness.

When we ask our heavenly Father for forgiveness, He gives it completely and without reservation. Then we must do the difficult work of forgiving ourselves in the same way God has forgiven us: thoroughly and unconditionally.

The Spanish writer Baltasar Gracián noted, "The things we remember best are those better forgotten." When you find that's true of your thoughts, it's time for a special kind of housecleaning—a cleansing of your mind and your heart.

> *Guilt is the gift that keeps on giving.*
> Erma Bombeck

Midcourse Corrections

*The prudent see danger and take refuge,
but the simple keep going and suffer for it.*
Proverbs 27:12 NIV

In our fast-paced world, everyday life has become an exercise in managing change. Our circumstances change; our relationships change; our bodies change. We grow older every day, as does our world. So what's a woman to do? The answer, of course, is to strive, as best she can, to make midcourse corrections when necessary.

The shifting tides of life have a way of testing our faith, our determination, and our common sense. But when we accept our changing circumstances and adapt to them, we gain maturity and insight.

Well-known speaker and author Karen Kaiser Clark said, "Life is change; growth is optional." You have the power to change—and to grow—every day of your life. Claim that power today.

Change is the only evidence of life.
Evelyn Waugh

Measuring Your Words

*A gentle answer turns away wrath,
but a harsh word stirs up anger.*
Proverbs 15:1 NIV

The Bible teaches us that "Reckless words pierce like a sword, but the tongue of the wise brings healing" (Proverbs 12:18 NIV). If we seek to be a source of encouragement to friends and family, then we must measure our words carefully. Words are important: they can hurt or heal. Words can uplift us or discourage us, and reckless words spoken in haste cannot be erased.

Today seek to encourage all who cross your path. Measure your words carefully. Speak wisely, not impulsively. Use words of kindness and praise, not words of anger or derision. Remember that you have the power to heal others or to injure them, to lift others up or to hold them back. When you lift them up, your words will bring healing and comfort to a world that needs both.

*The real art of conversation is not only to say
the right thing at the right place but to leave unsaid
the wrong thing at the tempting moment.*
Dorothy Nevill

The Direction of Your Thoughts

*Keep your eyes focused on what is right,
and look straight ahead to what is good.*
Proverbs 4:25 NCV

French poet Paul Valéry observed, "We hope vaguely but dread precisely." Too often we allow the worries of everyday life to overwhelm our thoughts and cloud our vision. What's needed is clearer perspective, renewed faith, and a different focus.

When we focus on the frustrations of today or the uncertainties of tomorrow, we rob ourselves of peace in the present moment. But when we direct our thoughts into more positive paths, we rob our worries of the power to tyrannize us.

Today remember that God is infinitely greater than the challenges you face. Remember also that your thoughts are profoundly powerful, so guard and direct them accordingly.

*Attitude is the mind's paintbrush;
it can color any situation.*
Barbara Johnson

When It's Hard to Decide

> *If you need wisdom—if you want to know what*
> *God wants you to do—ask him, and he will*
> *gladly tell you. He will not resent your asking.*
> James 1:5 NLT

Life presents each of us with countless questions, conundrums, doubts, and dilemmas. Perhaps Søren Kierkegaard was stating the obvious when he observed, "Life can only be understood backwards; but it must be lived forwards." Still, Kierkegaard's words are far easier to understand than they are to live by.

Taking a forward-looking approach to life means learning the art of solving problems and making decisions sensibly and consistently. Thankfully, the riddles of everyday living are not too difficult to solve if we look for answers in the right places. When we have questions, we can consult God's Word, our own consciences, and a few close friends and family members.

And then, when it's time to decide, we can decide.

> *No trumpets sound when the important decisions*
> *of our lives are made. Destiny is made known silently.*
> Agnes DeMille

Above and Beyond Bitterness

Don't insist on getting even; that's not for you to do.
"I'll do the judging," says God. "I'll take care of it."
Romans 12:19 MSG

Is someone you know mired in the quicksand of bitterness or regret? Are you? If so, it's worth noting that the world holds few, if any, rewards for those who remain angrily focused upon the past. Still, the act of forgiveness is often difficult.

Being frail, fallible, imperfect human beings, most of us are quick to anger, quick to blame, slow to forgive, and even slower to forget. Yet forgive we must.

If there exists even one person—alive or dead—against whom you hold bitter feelings, it's time to forgive. Or, if you are embittered against yourself for some past mistake, it's time to finally forgive yourself and move on. Why? Because you deserve the peace of mind that belongs to women (like you) who are wise enough to forgive.

The more a man knows, the more he forgives.
Catherine the Great

Becoming a Star

Commit to the LORD whatever you do,
and your plans will succeed.
Proverbs 16:3 NIV

In 1955 the Fulton Theater in New York was renamed the Helen Hayes Theater in honor of a unique woman who had, at the time, already spent fifty wonderful years on stage.

Ms. Hayes once advised, "Aim for achievement, and forget about success." Her advice was sound. If we spend too much time fretting over success, we won't spend enough time doing the things that ultimately make us successful.

So if you want to see your name up in lights, don't worry too much about who's getting top billing. Just play your role to the best of your ability, and while you're at it, don't worry too much about the critics—after all, if you're giving it your best effort, you're already a star.

Success is within your grasp.
If you believe it is possible,
you can make it happen.
Beatryce Nivens

Stumbling Blocks or Steppingstones?

In this world you will have trouble.
But take heart! I have overcome the world.
John 16:33 NIV

A lthough she lost her sight in infancy, she went on to become one of America's most beloved writers of religious poetry and hymns. She wrote more than nine thousand hymns; she spent her life teaching and serving the needy; and she became one of the most admired writers of the nineteenth century. Her name was Frances Crosby, better known to her legion of admirers as Fanny Crosby, the woman who penned the classic hymn "Blessed Assurance."

Fanny Crosby was never embittered by her blindness. To the contrary, she considered her handicap a steppingstone, not a stumbling block.

Can you find ways to turn your own stumbling blocks into steppingstones? Of course you can, and with God's help, you will.

Every problem comes gift wrapped in a package
that also contains a creative solution.
Your job is to accept both gifts.
Marie T. Freeman

Living Wisely

*Whoever listens to what is taught will succeed,
and whoever trusts the Lord will be happy.*

Proverbs 16:20 NCV

Wisdom is not like a mushroom; it does not spring up overnight. Rather, it's like an oak tree that starts as a tiny acorn, grows into a sapling, and eventually reaches up to the sky, tall and strong.

To become wise, we must seek wisdom in the right places, and we must apply the wisdom we find. We must seek out worthy mentors and listen carefully to their advice. We must associate, day in and day out, with sensible men and women. We must commit ourselves to a lifetime of learning. And we must act in accordance with our beliefs.

When we do these things, we will become wise—and we will be a blessing to our friends, to our families, and to the world.

*Wisdom is knowledge applied.
Head knowledge is useless on the battlefield.
Knowledge stamped on the heart makes one wise.*

Beth Moore

April

Beyond Anxiety

Be anxious for nothing, but in everything by
prayer and supplication with thanksgiving
let your requests be made known to God.
Philippians 4:6 NASB

When Dorothy Dix began answering readers' questions in her daily newspaper column, people loved it. And by 1939 she was the first lady of advice, with a syndicated column that reached sixty million readers. Dorothy had this advice about life: "Don't borrow trouble by dreading tomorrow. It's the dark menace of the future that makes cowards of us all."

If you've been wasting time and energy fretting about the consequences of some distant possibility, think again. After all, no one ever changed the future by dreading it. Instead of worrying about tomorrow, do today's work and leave everything up to God. When you do, you'll discover a peace that comes with knowing your todays and tomorrows are in the best hands possible.

Worry is as useless as a handle on a snowball.
Mitzi Chandler

Keeping Up Appearances

Man does not see what the Lord sees, for man sees what is visible, but the Lord sees the heart.
1 Samuel 16:7 HCSB

The world sees us as we appear to be; God sees us as we really are. He sees our hearts, and He understands our intentions. The opinions of others should be relatively unimportant to us; however, God's view of us—His understanding of our actions, our thoughts, and our motivations—should be vitally important.

The nineteenth-century reformer Margaret Fuller warned, "Beware of over-great pleasure in being popular or even beloved." And her words still ring true.

Few things in life are more futile than keeping up appearances for the sake of impressing the neighbors. So do yourself a favor: don't even try to keep up with the Joneses. You've got better things to do—far better things—like pleasing your loved ones here on earth and your Father in heaven.

Outside appearances, things like the clothes you wear or the car you drive, are important to other people but totally unimportant to God. When in doubt, trust God.
Marie T. Freeman

Rediscovering Hope

*We're not giving up. How could we! Even though
on the outside it often looks like things are falling apart
on us, on the inside, where God is making new life,
not a day goes by without his unfolding grace.*

2 Corinthians 4:16 MSG

She withdrew from society while in her twenties, but this reclusive young woman was not idle— she wrote poetry. After her death, some 1,800 of her poems were discovered—verses that are still admired today. Her name was Emily Dickinson, and she wrote, "Hope is the thing with feathers that perches in the soul."

Yet sometimes, when life flies out of control, it's tempting to abandon our hopes and dreams. Tempting, but wrong. So if you find yourself giving in to the twin evils of pessimism and doubt, it's time to reconsider. As Emily Dickinson would be quick to point out, hope is powerful medicine for the soul.

Make it your medicine.

*Far away in the sunshine are my highest aspirations.
I may not reach them, but I can look up
and see the beauty, believe in them,
and try to follow where they lead.*

Louisa May Alcott

It's Possible

If God be for us, who can be against us?
Romans 8:31 KJV

Cherilyn Sarkisian headed for Hollywood, dropped her last name altogether, and shortened her first name to, simply, Cher. Along the way she married songwriter Sonny Bono and became a glitzy Hollywood icon.

Cher once said, "If you really want something, you can figure out how to make it happen." Her words apply to you; if you're waiting for success to arrive, stop waiting and start working. Because, as the saying goes, there are three kinds of people: those who make things happen, those who wait for things to happen, and those who ask, "What happened?"

Wonderful things can happen when we put our minds and efforts to the task if our plans are within God's will.

The human race does command its own destination, and that destiny can eventually embrace the stars.
Lorraine Hansberry

God Can Handle It

The Lord is the One who will go before you.
He will be with you; He will not leave you or
forsake you. Do not be afraid or discouraged.
Deuteronomy 31:8 HCSB

Every human life is a tapestry of events: some grand, some not so grand, and some downright disheartening. When we reach the mountaintops of life, praising God is easy. In our moments of triumph, we trust God's plan. But when the storm clouds form overhead and we find ourselves in the dark valley of despair, our faith is stretched—sometimes to the breaking point. Yet we can take comfort: wherever we find ourselves, whether at the top of the mountain or the depths of the valley, God is there. And because He cares for us, we can live courageously.

You can call upon your Creator in your hour of need and find comfort. Whatever your challenge, whatever your trouble, God can handle it. And He will.

Our future may look fearfully intimidating,
yet we can look up to the Engineer of the Universe,
confident that nothing escapes His attention or
slips out of the control of those strong hands.
Elisabeth Elliot

Beyond Excuses

We must do the works of Him who sent Me while it is day. Night is coming when no one can work.
John 9:4 HCSB

Excuses are everywhere, and it's precisely because they're so prevalent that they're also so ineffective. When we hear the words, "I'm sorry but . . . ," most of us know exactly what's coming: an excuse. The dog ate the homework. Traffic was terrible. It's the teacher's fault. The boss is to blame. The equipment is broken. Yada yada yada.

All of the really good excuses have already been taken. In fact, the high-quality excuses have been used, reused, overused, and abused.

So next time you're tempted to spend time trying to concoct a new and improved excuse, don't bother. A far better strategy is this: do the work. And then let your work speak for itself.

If you don't want to do something, any excuse will do.
Author Unknown

Decisions, Decisions

*For the LORD gives wisdom; from His mouth
come knowledge and understanding.*
Proverbs 2:6 NKJV

We make countless decisions: decisions about the things we do, decisions about the words we speak, and decisions about the thoughts we entertain. Simply put, the quality of those choices determines the quality of our lives.

As you consider ways that decision making impacts your own life, take time to consider how many things in this life you can control: your thoughts, your words, your priorities, and your actions, for starters. Then, if you sincerely want to improve the quality of your life, learn to make the kind of choices that will enhance your life today, tomorrow, and in years to come.

To a large extent, your decisions will determine your future—so choose wisely.

*The location of your affections will
drive the direction of your decisions.*
Lisa Bevere

The Search for Significance

GOD *made everything with a place and purpose.*
Proverbs 16:4 MSG

In 1953 Elvis Presley was a wet-behind-the-ears high-school graduate who had just landed his first job, as a truck driver. One day, on a whim, he stopped his truck in front of a local recording studio and paid four dollars to record a song for his mother. A local producer heard the record and signed Elvis to a contract. The rest, of course, is rock-'n'-roll history. Within two years Elvis had become America's one-of-a-kind singing idol.

Elvis's philosophy was simple: he advised, "Do something worth remembering." He did, and you—in your own way and on your own stage—can too.

Novelist Willa Cather observed, "Life hurries past, too strong to stop, too sweet to lose." Life indeed hurries, but there's still time to do something significant—something nobody can do but you.

Nobody's gonna live for you.
Dolly Parton

Facing Life's Trials

Whatsoever is born of God overcometh the world.
1 John 5:4 KJV

All of us face times of adversity. When we face the inevitable difficulties of life here on earth, we can seek help from family, from friends, and from God—but not necessarily in that order.

Author Barbara Johnson wrote, "There is no way around suffering. We have to go through it to get to the other side." And the best way to get to the other side of suffering is to get there with God. When we turn to Him in heartfelt prayer, He will answer—in His own time and according to His own plan—and He will heal us.

And while we're waiting for God's plans to unfold and for His healing touch to restore us, we can be comforted in the knowledge that our Creator can overcome any obstacle, even if we cannot.

There are some things you learn best in calm, and some in storm.
Willa Cather

Ready, Set, Paddle!

When you pass through the waters, I will be with you.
Isaiah 43:2 NKJV

Katharine Hepburn was a surprisingly down-to-earth woman, one who was never blinded by the bright lights of Hollywood. And though she enjoyed a long-lasting and record-breaking career, she never rested on her laurels. Katharine said, "I've learned that as you go through life, if you don't paddle your own canoe, you don't move." And she was right.

So if you're waiting for the currents of life to carry you to safe harbor, it's probably time to reconsider. Your destination awaits, but life's waters are not always smooth. And as Ms. Hepburn would be quick to point out, if you want to sail off happily into the sunset, you'd better start paddling . . . oar else!

I say if it's going to be done, let's do it.
Let's not put it in the hands of fate.
Let's take a deep breath and go ahead.
Anita Baker

Overcoming the Disappointments

*"Peace to the far-off, peace to the near-at-hand,"
says God—"and yes, I will heal them."*
Isaiah 57:19 MSG

Some of our most important dreams are the ones we abandon. Some of our most important goals are the ones we don't attain. Sometimes our most important journeys are the ones we take to the winding conclusion of what seem to be dead-end streets. Thankfully, with God there are no dead ends; there are only opportunities to learn, to yield, to trust, to serve, and to grow.

The next time you experience one of life's inevitable disappointments, don't despair—and don't be afraid to try plan B. Consider every setback an opportunity to choose a new path. And as you take your next step, remember that what looks to you like a dead end may, in fact, be the fast lane according to God.

*The difference between winning and losing is
how we choose to react to disappointment.*
Barbara Johnson

April 12

Preparing for the Future

*Prepare your minds for service and have
self-control. All your hope should be
for the gift of grace that will be yours.*
1 Peter 1:13 NCV

Virginia Pugh was born in Mississippi with no silver
spoon in sight. She picked cotton, then worked as a
beautician while supporting three daughters. She lived
in a housing project, but she never gave up. Instead, she
started singing, changed her name to Tammy Wynette,
and cut a long string of country-music hits, including
"Stand by Your Man."

Tammy said, "If I hadn't faced tough times, I could
have never appreciated success." So the next time
you face a big challenge, remember young Virginia
Pugh. She made big plans and followed through—
and so can you. If you want to be a winner, follow
her example: plan for big things to happen, and then
stand by your plan.

*You don't arrive at a great performance
by a magical process. You arrive at it
by day-to-day slogging.*
Glenda Jackson

Your Real Riches

Your heart will be where your treasure is.
Luke 12:34 NCV

How important are our material possessions? Not as important as we might think. In a well-balanced life, material possessions should play a rather small role. Of course, we all need the basic necessities of life but once we meet those needs for ourselves and our families, the piling up of possessions often creates more problems than it solves. Our real riches are not of this world. We're never really rich until we are rich in spirit.

If you've become preoccupied with money and the stuff money can buy, it's time to de-emphasize material things and re-emphasize spiritual things. When you do, you'll begin storing up riches that will endure forever: the spiritual kind.

*I have held many things in my hands,
and I have lost them all; but whatever I have
placed in God's hands, that I still possess.*

Corrie ten Boom

Courage during Times of Change

> *Do not worry about tomorrow,*
> *for tomorrow will worry about itself.*
> *Each day has enough trouble of its own.*
> Matthew 6:34 NIV

When life unfolds according to our wishes, or when we experience unexpected good fortune, we find it easy to embrace change. We welcome it with open arms. But sometimes the changes we must endure are painful. When we struggle through the difficult days of life, as we must from time to time, we may ask, "Why me?" The answer, of course, is that God knows—but He isn't telling . . . yet.

Have you endured a difficult transition that has left your head spinning or your heart broken? If so, you have a clear choice to make: you can cry and complain, or you can trust God and allow Him to fix what's broken. The former is a formula for disaster; the latter is a formula for a well-lived life.

> *The key to change . . . is to let go of fear.*
> *Rosanne Cash*

A Passionate Life

He did it with all his heart. So he prospered.
2 Chronicles 31:21 NKJV

We have every reason to be enthusiastic about life, but sometimes the struggles of daily living may cause us to feel decidedly unenthusiastic. Whenever we feel our energies begin to fade, it's time to slow down, to rest, to count our blessings, and to have a sensible talk with God. When we feel worried or weary, a few moments spent in quiet conversation with the Creator can calm our fears and restore our perspective.

Gymnastics champion Mary Lou Retton said, "Heat is required to forge anything. Every great accomplishment is the story of a flaming heart." Is your heart aflame? Are you fully engaged in life? If so, keep up the good work! But if you feel the passion slowly draining from your life, it's time to refocus your thoughts, your energies, and your prayers so you can live life to the fullest.

To love what you do and feel that it matters—
how could anything be more fun?
Katharine Graham

Looking Inside

*You created my inmost being; you knit me together
in my mother's womb. I praise you because
I am fearfully and wonderfully made.*
Psalm 139:13–14 NIV

Suzanne Somers's Hollywood career had been stuck in neutral when she accepted a role as a mysterious blonde driving a sports car in the movie *American Graffiti*. That role jump-started her career and propelled her to stardom on television, on stage, and as a popular spokesperson for fitness gadgets.

In looking back over a life of ups and downs, Suzanne also spent time looking inward. She said, "Self-examination made me a better person. I look back on the experience not only as a positive one . . . but as a gift."

If you'd like to get your inner self in shape, take a fitness tip from Suzanne and slow down long enough to examine your life and your priorities. If you take time to recharge your batteries, you can jump-start your life.

*Never be afraid to look at yourself
as carefully as you look at other people.*
Author Unknown

Embracing the One Who Embraces Us

*I will sing of the LORD's great love forever;
with my mouth I will make your faithfulness
known through all generations.*

Psalm 89:1 NIV

Christian apologist C. S. Lewis observed, "A person's spiritual health is exactly proportional to his love for God." If we are to enjoy the spiritual health God intends for us, we should keep Lewis's words in mind.

In seeking that spiritual health by developing our love for God, it also will help us to remember something Corrie ten Boom said: "A bird does not know it can fly before it uses its wings. We learn God's love in our hearts as soon as we act upon it." She understood that whenever we worship God with our hearts and our minds, we are blessed by our love for Him and His love for us.

Today let us embrace the One who embraces us. He deserves no less.

Life in God is a great big hug that lasts forever!

Barbara Johnson

Say Cheese!

What a relief it is to see your friendly smile.
It is like seeing the smile of God!
Genesis 33:10 NLT

After marrying and spending fifteen years raising five kids, one woman hatched an ambitious career goal: stand-up comedy. It took five years on the nightclub circuit before she began appearing on television in outrageous outfits and crazy hairstyles, but eventually Phyllis Diller became one of America's most recognizable comics. Her philosophy was, "A smile is a curve that sets everything straight."

If you want to set things straight in your life, do yourself a favor—try the Phyllis Diller formula for happiness: smile. You'll discover that smiles, like laughter, are contagious. The more you smile, the better you (and the people near you) will feel. And as funny lady Phyllis would surely agree, that's no joke.

Every time you smile at someone,
it is an action of love,
a gift to that person, a beautiful thing.
Mother Teresa

The Shepherd's Care

Be strong and brave, and do the work.
Don't be afraid or discouraged, because the LORD God,
my God, is with you. He will not fail you or leave you.
1 Chronicles 28:20 NCV

God is like a shepherd, continually watching His flock, searching for lost sheep, seeking those who need protection, guidance, and salvation.

God loves us and protects us. In times of trouble, He comforts us; in times of sorrow, He dries our tears. Sometimes we may feel lost or afraid, but we're never alone; the face of God is always turned toward us. Proverbs 5:21 promises, "The LORD sees everything you do, and he watches where you go" (NCV).

Remember that God is as near as your next breath. So trust Him and turn to Him for solace and security.

He goes before us, follows behind us,
and hems us safe inside the realm of His protection.
Beth Moore

An Imperfect and Wonderful Life

*We are troubled on every side, yet not distressed;
we are perplexed, but not in despair.*
2 Corinthians 4:8 KJV

In the 1950s Annette Funicello was the most glamorous member of television's *The Mickey Mouse Club*. After the club closed its TV doors, she went on to star in a string of Disney movies. But Annette's star shone most brightly thirty years after she hung up her Mickey Mouse ears—when she was diagnosed with multiple sclerosis.

Discussing her illness, Annette said, "Life does not have to be perfect to be wonderful." We should take her courageous words to heart. Whether life has thrown you a curve ball or you're just having a tough day, take a tip from Annette and remember that it's a wonderful life. Even during the toughest times, you'll see that your blessings are still too numerous to count.

*I have always grown from my problems
and challenges, from the things that don't work out;
that's when I've really learned.*
Carol Burnett

April 21

Outside the Comfort Zone

*God doesn't want us to be shy with his gifts,
but bold and loving and sensible.*
2 Timothy 1:7 MSG

Risk is an inevitable fact of life. From the moment we arise in the morning until the moment we drift off to sleep at night, we face a wide array of risks, both great and small.

Some risks, of course, should be avoided at costs—these include risky behaviors that drive us further and further away from God's will for our lives. Yet other risks—the kinds of risks that we must take in order to expand our horizons and expand our faith—should be accepted as the inevitable price we must pay for living full and productive lives.

Have you planted yourself firmly inside your own comfort zone? If so, it's time to reconsider the direction and scope of your activities. God has big plans for you, but those plans will most likely require you to expand your comfort zone—or leave it altogether.

The idea of always playing it safe, never venturing out of our comfort zone, and refusing to broaden the borders of our experience is stultifying.
Marilyn Meberg

Transforming Power

Do not be conformed to this world, but be transformed by the renewing of your mind, that you may prove what is that good and acceptable and perfect will of God.
Romans 12:2 NKJV

God has the power to transform our lives. Our choice is straightforward: whether or not to allow the Father's transforming power to work in us and through us. God stands at the door and waits; all we must do is knock. When we do, God always answers.

Sometimes the demands of daily life may seem overwhelming, but even during the most difficult of days, we can be comforted in the knowledge that God has the power to renew our spirit and our lives.

Are you in need of a new beginning? Is it time for a fresh start? If you want to change, you can do it—and God is ready to help. In fact, the creator of the universe is in the business of making all things new—including you.

God's work is not in buildings, but in transformed lives.
Ruth Bell Graham

Restoring Confidence

You are my hope; O Lord God,
You are my confidence.
Psalm 71:5 NASB

Doubts come in several shapes and sizes: doubts about God, about the future, and about our own abilities, for starters. But when doubts creep in, as they will from time to time, we need not despair. As singer and author Sheila Walsh observed, "To wrestle with God does not mean that we have lost faith, but that we are fighting for it."

God never leaves our side, not for an instant. He is always with us, always willing to calm the storms of life. When we sincerely seek His presence—and when we genuinely seek to establish a deeper, more meaningful relationship with Him—God is prepared to touch our hearts, to calm our fears, to answer our doubts, and to restore our confidence.

As I have grown in faith and confidence,
I have known more and more that my worth
is based on the love of God.
Leslie Williams

Infinite Possibilities

Glory be to God! By his mighty power at work within us, he is able to accomplish infinitely more than we would ever dare to ask or hope.
Ephesians 3:20 NLT

We live in a world of infinite possibilities. But sometimes, because of limited faith and limited understanding, we wrongly assume that God cannot or will not intervene in the affairs of mankind. Such assumptions are simply wrong.

Are you afraid to ask God to do big things in your life? Is your faith threadbare and worn? If so, it's time to abandon your doubts and reclaim your faith—faith in God's promises and faith in what your heavenly Father can do through you.

Noted author and speaker Catherine Marshall said, "God specializes in things thought impossible." Make no mistake: God can help you do things you never dreamed possible. Your job is to let Him.

If you believe in a God who controls the big things, you have to believe in a God who controls the little things. It is we, of course, to whom things look "little" or "big."
Elisabeth Elliot

Trusting God's Timetable

He has made everything beautiful in its time.
Also He has put eternity in their hearts.
Ecclesiastes 3:11 NKJV

We should learn to trust God's timing, but we're sorely tempted to do otherwise. Why? Because we humans are usually anxious for things to happen sooner rather than later. But God knows better.

God has created a world that unfolds according to His own timetable, not ours—thank goodness! We mortals would make a terrible mess of things. God does not. His plan does not always happen in the way we would like or at the time of our choosing. But our task is to wait patiently and never lose hope.

In the words of Elisabeth Elliot, "We must learn to move according to the timetable of the Timeless One, and to be at peace." That's advice worth following today, tomorrow, and every day.

God's delays and His ways can be confusing because
the process God uses to accomplish His will can
go against human logic and common sense.
Anne Graham Lotz

Opportunities to Encourage

*Encourage one another and build
each other up as you are already doing.*
1 Thessalonians 5:11 HCSB

Barnabas (an early follower of Jesus whose name meant "Son of Encouragement") was known for his kindness and for his ability to encourage others. Today, as citizens of a difficult world, we must seek to imitate the "Son of Encouragement."

We imitate Barnabas when we offer hugs and kind words to our loved ones. We imitate Barnabas when our actions give credence to our beliefs. We imitate Barnabas when we are generous with our possessions and with our praise. We imitate Barnabas when we give hope to the hopeless and encouragement to the downtrodden.

Today we, like Barnabas, can literally change the world one person—and one hug—at a time. And that's precisely what we should do.

*Giving encouragement to others is a most
welcome gift, for the results of it are lifted spirits,
increased self-worth, and a hopeful future.*
Florence Littauer

Accepting His Blessings and Giving Thanks

Thou, LORD, wilt bless the righteous.
Psalm 5:12 KJV

If you sat down and began counting your blessings, how long would it take? Probably a very, very long time! Your blessings likely include a life, freedom, family, friends, talents, and possessions, and the list goes on and on.

Give thanks today for your blessings by accepting them fully (with open arms) and by sharing them generously (with a thankful heart).

Evangelist Billy Graham had this advice: "Think of the blessings we so easily take for granted: life itself; preservation from danger; every bit of health we enjoy; every hour of liberty; the ability to see, to hear, to speak, to think, and to imagine. All this comes from the hand of God." Meditating on our blessings and giving thanks is sound advice for all of us, who have been blessed beyond measure.

God is always far more willing to give us good things than we are anxious to have them.
Catherine Marshall

When God Seems Far Away

The Lord is with you when you are with Him.
If you seek Him, He will be found by you.
2 Chronicles 15:2 HCSB

If God is everywhere, why does He sometimes seem far away? The answer to that question, of course, has nothing to do with God and everything to do with us.

When we begin each day by thanking God for another day of life, the Creator often seems near indeed. But if we allow ourselves to become so busy that we ignore God's presence or—worse yet—rebel against it, the world in which we live becomes spiritually desolate.

In whatever condition you happen to find yourself—happy or sad, victorious or vanquished, troubled or triumphant—celebrate God's presence and be comforted. He is never far away. In fact, He is right here, right now. And He wants to help you.

God walks with us. He scoops us up
in His arms or simply sits with us in silent strength
until we cannot avoid the awesome recognition
that yes, even now, He is here.
Gloria Gaither

Finding Someone to Help

*Those of us who are strong and able in the faith need
to step in and lend a hand to those who falter. . . .
Each one of us needs to look after the good of the people
around us, asking ourselves, "How can I help?"*

Romans 15:1–2 MSG

In 1991 Naomi Judd faced a life-threatening case
of hepatitis C and reluctantly retired from country
music. But she didn't retire from life. Gradually, as her
health began to improve, she poured more time and
effort into volunteer work. Today Naomi supports
a wide range of charities, and she believes that her
philanthropy has actually helped in her own healing.
She said, "Helping other people gives me the same kind
of physical and emotional charge as singing in Madison
Square Garden. It has helped me heal."

The next time you're feeling a little low, try
Naomi's prescription: find someone to help. That
person will feel better, and so will you.

A willing helper doesn't wait until she is asked.

Old Saying

Work, Work, Work

The people had a mind to work.
Nehemiah 4:6 KJV

One young woman began her music career in hotel foyers, singing for spare change wherever her rodeo-champion father was competing. Eventually she even rode horses in barrel-racing events. But in 1974, while singing the national anthem at the Rodeo Finals in Oklahoma, at last Reba McEntire was discovered by a music-industry executive. What followed was an incredible string of country-music hits.

Years later, Reba's advice for young performers was straightforward: "Be different, stand out, and work, work, work!" That's wonderful advice for you, even if you never set foot on stage. If you want to top the charts at work, home, or school, stand out by working smarter and harder. When you do, the results will be solid gold.

God has a plan for all of us,
but He expects us to do our share of the work.
Minnie Pearl

May

Marriage and Commitment

Let love and faithfulness never leave you. . . .
Write them on the tablet of your heart.
Proverbs 3:3 NIV

The Bible makes it clear: love and commitment are to be intertwined. That's especially necessary in a marriage relationship. Unfortunately, we live in a world where marriage vows are taken too lightly. Too many couples are far too quick to push the panic button—or the eject button—and the results are both predictable and unfortunate.

When we vow to love our partner "till death do us part," we must take that promise seriously. And we'd better be willing to do the hard work required to make the marriage last.

If you're a married woman (or if you're thinking about becoming one), please take the advice of Proverbs 3:3 seriously: write the words love and faithfulness on the tablet of your heart. And be sure to use permanent ink!

Marriages may be made in heaven, but a lot of the details have to be worked out here on earth.
Gloria Pitzer

Letting God Decide

*I will instruct you and teach you in the way
you should go; I will guide you with My eye.*
Psalm 32:8 NKJV

Sometimes we all face problems that defy easy
solutions. If you find yourself facing a difficult
decision, here's a simple formula for making the right
choice: let God decide. Instead of fretting about the
future, pray about it.

When you consult your heavenly Father early and
often, you'll soon discover that the quiet moments
you spend with Him can be very helpful. God will
quietly lead you along a path of His choosing, a path
that is right for you.

So the next time you arrive at one of life's
inevitable crossroads, take a moment or two to have
a chat with the Ultimate Advisor. When you do,
you'll never stay lost for long.

*Are you serious about wanting God's guidance to
become a personal reality in your life? The first step
is to tell God that you know you can't manage
your own life; that you need His help.*
Catherine Marshall

The World and You

The mind-set of the flesh is death,
but the mind-set of the Spirit is life and peace.
Romans 8:6 HCSB

We live in the world, but we shouldn't worship it. Yet at every turn, or so it seems, we're tempted to do just that—because, as author Warren Wiersbe correctly observed, "the world is deceptive, it is dangerous."

The twenty-first-century world we live in is a noisy, distracting place—a place that offers countless temptations and dangers. The world seems to cry out, "Worship me with your time, your money, your energy, your thoughts, and your life!" But if we're wise, we won't fall prey to that temptation.

C. S. Lewis said, "Aim at heaven and you will get earth thrown in; aim at earth and you will get neither." That's good advice. You're likely to hit what you aim at, so aim high. Aim at heaven.

I have a divided heart, trying to love God
and the world at the same time.
God says, "You can't love Me
as you should if you love this world too."
Mary Morrison Suggs

Defeating Discouragement

*Be strong; don't be discouraged,
for your work has a reward.*
2 Chronicles 15:7 HCSB

When we fail to meet the expectations of others (or, for that matter, the expectations we have for ourselves), we may be tempted to abandon hope. Thankfully, on those cloudy days when our strength is sapped and our faith is shaken, there exists a God from whom we can draw courage and wisdom.

Isaiah 40:31 teaches us that "those who wait on the LORD shall renew their strength; they shall mount up with wings like eagles, they shall run and not be weary, they shall walk and not faint" (NKJV).

So if you're feeling defeated or discouraged, remember Isaiah's words and think of the following advice from Mrs. Charles E. Cowman, compiler of the popular book *Streams in the Desert*: "Never yield to gloomy anticipation. Place your hope and confidence in God. He has no record of failure."

*The most profane word we use is "hopeless."
When you say a situation or person is hopeless,
you are slamming the door in the face of God.*
Kathy Troccoli

Hugs for Our Children

Lay up these words of mine in your heart and in your soul. . . . Teach them to your children, speaking of them when you sit in your house, when you walk by the way, when you lie down, and when you rise up.

Deuteronomy 11:18–19 NKJV

Have you hugged a child lately? If so, you've experienced one of life's great pleasures. Every child is a priceless gift from the Creator. And when we share love and affection with our children, we—and they—are blessed beyond measure.

As parents, friends of parents, aunts, and grandmothers, we understand the critical importance of raising our children with love, with discipline, and with God. It's a tall order and a profoundly important responsibility. But with God's help, we can do it.

Every child needs the presence of caring adults who serve as positive role models. May we, as concerned adults, behave ourselves—and raise our children—accordingly.

A child's hand in yours—what tenderness it arouses, what power it conjures. You are instantly the very touchstone of wisdom and strength.

Marjorie Holmes

Working Miracles

My heart took delight in all my work.
Ecclesiastes 2:10 NIV

In 1887 Anne Sullivan became the governess of a young girl named Helen Keller. Helen had been left blind and deaf by a childhood illness, but Anne started teaching and little Helen started learning. Anne became known as "the miracle worker," but she knew that Keller's improvement wasn't a miracle at all. It was the result of dedication, perseverance, and good old-fashioned hard work. Anne noted, "People seldom see the halting and painful steps by which real success is achieved."

If you've been impatient for your own success, remember that your giant leap forward may be preceded by a lengthy succession of short, halting steps. But keep the faith, keep working, and keep taking those steps, even if they're small ones. If you do, the results might just be miraculous.

Love is the divine reality that everywhere produces and restores life. To each and every one of us, it gives the power of working miracles if we will.
Lydia Maria Child

Use It or Lose It

Do not neglect the spiritual gift within you.
1 Timothy 4:14 NASB

She was born Erma Louise Fiste, but she was much better known to fans by her married name, Erma Bombeck. Erma began her writing career working for a small, local newspaper in Ohio. But with hard work and talent, she moved steadily to the top.

Shortly before her death in 1996, Erma Bombeck wrote, "When I stand before God at the end of my life, I would hope that I have not a single bit of talent left and could say, 'Lord, I used everything you gave me.'"

Like Erma Bombeck, you are blessed with special gifts. And as the old saying goes, "Talent is God's gift to you—how you use it is your gift to God." If Erma were here, she'd advise you to use your talent wisely, courageously, and often—starting now.

God has given you special talents—
now it's your turn to give them back to God.
Marie T. Freeman

Safest and Best

*It is God who is at work in you, both to will
and to work for His good pleasure.*
Philippians 2:13 NASB

Whether you realize it or not, God is busily working in you and through you. He has things He wants you to do and people He wants you to help. Your assignment, should you choose to accept it, is to seek God's will and to follow it.

Elisabeth Elliot said, "I believe that in every time and place it is within our power to acquiesce in the will of God—and what peace it brings to do so!" And Corrie ten Boom observed, "Surrendering to the Lord is not a tremendous sacrifice, not an agonizing performance. It is the most sensible thing you can do."

So as you make plans for the future, make sure your plans conform to God's plans—that's the safest and best way to live.

*The only safe place is in the center of God's will.
It is not only the safest place. It is also the most
rewarding and the most satisfying place to be.*
Gigi Graham Tchividjian

Hugs for Friends and Family

Friends come and friends go,
but a true friend sticks by you like family.
Proverbs 18:24 MSG

A loving family is a treasure from God; so is a trustworthy friend. If you're a member of a close-knit, supportive clan, offer a word of thanks to your Creator. And if you have a close circle of trustworthy, huggable friends, consider yourself richly blessed.

Today let us praise God for our family and for our friends. God has placed these people along our paths. Let us love them, encourage them, hug them, and care for them. And let's give thanks to the Father for all the people who enrich our lives. They are, in a very real sense, gifts from God. We should treat them as such.

What a great favor God does to those whom
He places in the company of good people!
Saint Teresa of Avila

Faith versus Fear

Be not afraid, only believe.
Mark 5:36 KJV

As we consider the uncertainties of the future, we are confronted with a powerful temptation to play it safe. Unwilling to move mountains, we fret over molehills. Unwilling to entertain great hopes for tomorrow, we focus on the unfairness of today. Unwilling to trust God completely, we take timid half steps when He intends for us to take giant leaps.

Ask God today for the courage to step beyond the boundaries of your doubts. Ask Him to guide you to a place where you can realize your full potential—a place where you are freed from the fear of failure. Don't ask Him to lead you to a safe place; ask Him to lead you to the right place. And remember, those two places are seldom the same.

*Become so wrapped up in something
that you forget to be afraid.*
Lady Bird Johnson

His Quiet Presence

The eyes of the LORD are in every place, keeping watch.
Proverbs 15:3 NKJV

We live in a fast-paced world where the demands of everyday life can seem overwhelming at times. But when we slow down and seek the presence of a loving God, we invite His peace into our hearts.

When we set aside quiet moments each day to collect our thoughts and praise our Creator, we gain faith, courage, and wisdom. As busy author Janette Oke observed, "A quiet morning with God puts the events of the upcoming day into proper perspective."

The words of Psalm 46:10 remind us to "be still, and know that I am God" (NKJV). When we do so, we encounter the quiet presence of our heavenly Father—and we're comforted in the knowledge that God is not just near. He is here.

The love of God is so vast, the power of His touch so invigorating, we could just stay in His presence for hours, soaking up His glory, basking in His blessings.
Debra Evans

The Right Kind of Example

*Set an example of good works yourself,
with integrity and dignity in your teaching.*
Titus 2:7 HCSB

Born in 1860, Jane Addams was a tireless worker for social change. By the time she won the Nobel Peace Prize in 1931, many considered her to be America's most prominent woman. This exemplary woman believed, "Our future is determined by the home and the school. The child becomes largely what he is taught, so we must watch what we teach, and how we live."

Jane understood that at home, work, or school, our actions always speak far more loudly than our words. So if you want to make your mark on the world, talk less and do more. You may not win a Nobel Prize, but you will win the hearts and minds of family, friends, coworkers, and just as importantly, you'll win approval from yourself.

*Life is not easy for any of us. But it is a continual
challenge, and it is up to us to be cheerful and
to be strong, so that those who depend on us
may draw strength from our example.*
Rose Kennedy

Choosing the Good Life

"Well done, good and faithful servant!
You have been faithful with a few things;
I will put you in charge of many things.
Come and share your master's happiness!"
Matthew 25:21 NIV

God offers us abundance, but He does not force abundance upon us.

When we entrust our hearts and our days to the one who created us, we experience abundance through His grace. But when we turn our thoughts and direct our energies away from God, we inevitably forfeit the spiritual abundance that might otherwise be ours.

When we sincerely seek the riches our God offers to those who give themselves to Him and then follow Him completely and without reservation, we will participate in the good life the Shepherd offers His sheep. It is your choice to accept it.

God has promised us abundance and peace.
One of the great mysteries of life is
why on earth do so many of us wait
so very long to lay claim to God's gifts?
Marie T. Freeman

Finding Purpose Now

*All things work together for good to those
who love God, to those who are the called
according to His purpose.*
Romans 8:28 NKJV

Life is best lived on purpose. And purpose, like
everything else in the universe, begins with God.
Whether we realize it or not, God has a plan for our
lives—a divine calling, a direction in which He is
leading us. When we welcome God into our hearts
and establish a genuine relationship with Him, He
will begin, in time, to make His purposes known.

Sometimes God's intentions will be clear to us;
other times His plan will seem uncertain at best.
But even on those difficult days when we're not sure
which way to turn, we must never lose sight of these
overriding facts: God created us for a reason; He
has important work for us to do; and He's waiting
patiently for us to do it.

*The one predominant duty is to
find one's work and to do it.*
Charlotte Perkins Gilman

Joy to the World

Let the hearts of those who seek the LORD rejoice.
Look to the LORD and his strength; seek his face always.
1 Chronicles 16:10–11 NIV

Martha's husband, a man named Daniel Custis, had died, and Martha was left to raise her two surviving children alone. Two years later she remarried, this time to a man named George Washington, and the former Mrs. Custis became Martha Washington, America's first First Lady.

Despite the tragedies in her life, Martha remained optimistic. She said, "We carry the seeds of happiness with us wherever we go." And she was right.

So the next time you're feeling blue, remember that wherever you go, you carry within you the potential to be joyful. Realizing that potential is up to you, but it's always there. You possess the seeds of happiness. Plant them.

Joy is not gush; joy is not mere jolliness.
Joy is perfect acquiescence, acceptance,
and rest in God's will, whatever comes.
Amy Carmichael

Touching the Future

Don't be in any rush to become a teacher, my friends.
Teaching is highly responsible work.
Teachers are held to the strictest standards.
James 3:1 MSG

Chosen from eleven thousand applicants to be the first teacher in space, a high-school social-studies teacher strode aboard the shuttle *Challenger* with her crewmates on January 28, 1986. And so it was that Christa McAuliffe perished on that fateful day when the *Challenger* exploded in midair.

Before her first and final shuttle flight, Christa said, "I touch the future. I teach." And so should we. We teach whenever we serve as role models to those around us. We teach whenever we share a kind word, a sincere prayer, or a heartfelt hug. In a very real sense, we are all teachers, and we should behave accordingly.

Whether you teach in the classroom or outside it, be sure that both your message and your example are up to the challenge, because people of all ages are watching.

Teachers, I believe, are the most responsible and
important members of society because their
professional efforts affect the fate of the earth.
Helen Caldicott

The Treasure Hunt

The one who loves money is never satisfied
with money, and whoever loves wealth [is]
never [satisfied] with income. This too is futile.
Ecclesiastes 5:10 HCSB

All of mankind is engaged in a colossal, worldwide treasure hunt. Some people seek treasure from earthly sources, treasures such as material wealth or public acclaim; others seek God's treasures by making Him the cornerstone of their lives.

What kind of treasure hunter are you? Are you so caught up in the demands of everyday living that you sometimes allow the search for worldly treasures to become your primary focus? If so, it's time to think long and hard about what you value and why.

All the items on your daily to-do list are not created equal. That's why you must do the hard work of putting first things first. And the "first things" in life definitely have less to do with material riches than with riches of the spiritual kind.

We are made spiritually lethargic
by a steady diet of materialism.
Mary Morrison Suggs

At Peace with Your Purpose

God has called us to live in peace.
1 Corinthians 7:15 NIV

Are you at peace with the direction of your life? Or are you still rushing after the illusion of peace and happiness that our world promises but cannot deliver? The answer to this simple question will determine, to a surprising extent, the direction and the quality of your day and your life.

Popular speaker and author Joyce Meyer said, "We need to be at peace with our past, content with our present, and sure about our future, knowing they are all in God's hands."

Today, as a gift to yourself, to your family, and to your friends, claim the inner peace that is your spiritual birthright. It is offered freely; it's yours for the asking. So ask—and then share.

We plant seeds that will flower as results in our lives, so best to remove the weeds of anger, avarice, envy and doubt, that peace and abundance may manifest for all.
Dorothy Day

Think Rich

Do everything without complaining or arguing.
Then you will be innocent and without any wrong.
Philippians 2:14–15 NCV

Doris von Kappelhoff dreamed of becoming a dancer, but an automobile crash left her dreams in shambles. So she turned instead to singing. Along the way Doris changed her last name, borrowing from the song "Day by Day." So Doris von Kappelhoff became Doris Day . . . and Doris Day became one of the biggest movie stars of the 1950s and 1960s.

Doris once said, "Gratitude is riches. Complaint is poverty." And her words apply to all of us. Chronic complaining—a rather common malady that infects all of us from time to time—solves nothing. So let's give thanks for blessings past, present, and future. As Doris von Kappelhoff proved, it takes great thoughts to make a great day (or, for that matter, a great Day).

You don't make progress by standing
on the sidelines, whimpering and complaining.
You make progress by implementing ideas.
Shirley Chisholm

Great Is Thy Faithfulness

*Let us hold on to the confession of our hope
without wavering, for He who promised is faithful.*
Hebrews 10:23 HCSB

God is faithful to us even when we're not faithful to Him. God keeps His promises to us even when we stray far from His path. God offers us countless blessings, but He does not force His blessings upon us. If we are to experience His love and His grace, we must claim them for ourselves.

God is with you today. Listen prayerfully to the quiet voice of your heavenly Father. Talk with God often; seek His guidance; watch for His signs; listen to the wisdom He shares through the voice of your own conscience.

God loves you and wants you to have all the best He has to offer. You can claim His blessings today by being faithful to Him.

*God is always faithful to us . . .
and we, in turn, must be faithful to Him.*
Sheila Walsh

With a Hug and a Smile

*Go after a life of love as if
your life depended on it—because it does.*
1 Corinthians 14:1 MSG

This world can be a difficult place, a place where many of our friends and family members are troubled by the inevitable challenges of everyday life. And since we can never be certain who needs our help, we should be careful to speak helpful words to everyone who crosses our paths.

The apostle Paul wrote, "Do not let any unwholesome talk come out of your mouths, but only what is helpful for building others up according to their needs, that it may benefit those who listen" (Ephesians 4:29 NIV). Paul reminds us that when we choose our words carefully, we can have a powerful impact on those around us.

Today let's share kind words, smiles, encouragement, and hugs with family, with friends, and with the world.

*A smile is the light in the window of
your face that tells people you're at home.*
Barbara Johnson

A Pearl of Wisdom

*Enter his gates with thanksgiving, go into his courts
with praise. Give thanks to him and bless his name.*
Psalm 100:4 NLT

Pearl Bailey's singing career spanned six decades, and she received a Presidential Medal of Freedom. This notable woman said, "A person without ambition is dead. A person with ambition but no love is dead. But a person with ambition and love for his blessings here on earth is ever so alive."

Today you'll do yourself a favor if you put Pearl Bailey's pearl of wisdom into practice: be ambitious and count your blessings. When you're willing to work for your blessings—and count them—there's no limit on how far you can go, and no limit on the fun you'll have getting there.

*Feeling grateful or appreciative of someone or
something in your life actually attracts more of
the things that you appreciate and value into your life.
And the more of your life that you like and
appreciate, the healthier you'll be.*
Christiane Northrup

Never Alone

In all things approving ourselves as
the ministers of God, in much patience,
in afflictions, in necessities, in distresses.
2 Corinthians 6:4 KJV

Women of every generation have experienced adversity, and this generation is no different. But today's women face challenges that previous generations scarcely could have imagined. Thankfully, although the world continues to change, God's love remains constant. He remains ready to comfort us and strengthen us whenever we turn to Him.

Counselor and author Paula Rinehart advised, "If you want to know real joy in life, then be willing to let pain tutor your soul." When we face up to suffering, we grow spiritually and emotionally.

When we encounter troubles, of whatever kind, if we call upon God, in time He will heal us. And until He does, we can be comforted in the knowledge that we never suffer alone.

The love of God exists in its strongest and purest
form in the very midst of suffering and tragedy.
Suzanne Dale Ezell

God's Power to Heal

*The Lord says, "Peace, peace to the one
who is far or near, and I will heal him."*
Isaiah 57:19 HCSB

Are you concerned about your spiritual, physical,
or emotional health? If so, a timeless source of
comfort and assurance is as near as your next breath.
That source of comfort, of course, is God.

God is concerned about every aspect of your life,
including your health. When you face concerns of
any kind—including health-related challenges—
God is with you. So trust your medical doctor
to do his or her part, and turn to your family and
friends for moral, physical, and spiritual support. But
don't be afraid to place your ultimate trust in your
benevolent heavenly Father. His healing touch, like
His love, endures forever.

*If you want to receive emotional healing from God
and come into an area of wholeness, you must realize
that healing is a process, and you must allow
the Lord to deal with you and your problem
in His own way and in His own time.*
Joyce Meyer

A Prescription for Panic

Cast all your anxiety on him because he cares for you.
1 Peter 5:7 NIV

Our world seems to invite panic. Everywhere we turn we're met with disturbing images that cry out, "All is lost." But with God all is never lost; there is always hope.

God calls us to live above and beyond anxiety. He calls us to live by faith, not by fear. He instructs us to trust Him completely, this day and forever. But sometimes trusting God is difficult, especially when we get caught up in the incessant demands of an anxious world.

When you feel anxious—and you will—return your thoughts to God's love. Then take your concerns to Him in prayer and, to the best of your ability, leave them there. Whatever "it" is, God is big enough to handle it. Let Him.

Worry is a cycle of inefficient thoughts
whirling around a center of fear.
Corrie ten Boom

Hugs in the Here and Now

*Are there those among you who are truly wise
and understanding? Then they should show it
by living right and doing good things with
a gentleness that comes from wisdom.*
James 3:13 NCV

Do you know someone who needs a hug (or a smile, or a kind word) right now? If so, it's up to you to do something right now—not tomorrow, not next week—now. True, you may be a busy woman whose calendar is full. You may have many obligations, a long to-do list, and many people to care for. No matter. You should share love today, not wait until some point in the distant future.

When it comes to planting God's seeds in the soil of eternity, the only certain time we have is now. And when it comes to sharing hugs with our family and friends, there's simply no time like the present.

Exhaust the little moment. Soon it dies.
Gwendolyn Brooks

Beyond Blame

*People's own foolishness ruins their lives,
but in their minds they blame the Lord.*
Proverbs 19:3 NCV

To blame others for our own problems is the height of futility. Yet blaming others is a favorite human pastime. Why? Because blaming is much easier than fixing. So instead of solving our problems legitimately (by doing the work required to solve them), we're inclined to fret, to blame, and to criticize while doing precious little else. When we do, our problems quite predictably remain unsolved.

Have you acquired the bad habit of blaming others for problems you could or should solve yourself? If so, you're wasting precious time and energy. Take a moment to consider the possibility that you are at least partly responsible for the problem. But whether or not you bear any responsibility for the problem, remember that focusing on a solution instead of whose fault it is will get you to your desired result much faster and will be healthier for your heart and soul.

*You'll never win the blame game,
so why even bother to play?*
Marie T. Freeman

First Things First

*Seek first the kingdom of God and His righteousness,
and all these things will be provided for you.*
Matthew 6:33 HCSB

Have you fervently asked God to help prioritize your life? If so, you're inviting Him to become a full-fledged partner in your endeavors.

When you make God's priorities your priorities, you will receive His abundance and His peace. When you allow God control in every aspect of your life, He will lead you along the proper path: His path. When you allow God to play a role in the organization of your day, He'll honor you with spiritual blessings too numerous to count. So as you plan for the day ahead, take a few quiet moments to gather your thoughts and consult your Creator. It's the best way to plan your day and your life.

*Jesus's life was a constant demonstration
that there are only two things
that matter in this life: God and people.
They are the only things that last forever.*
Rebecca Manley Pippert

One-of-a-Kind Opportunities to Serve

*For we are God's workmanship, created
in Christ Jesus to do good works,
which God prepared in advance for us to do.*
Ephesians 2:10

You're a special person, created by God, and He has unique work for you to do. Do you acknowledge your own uniqueness, and do you celebrate the one-of-kind opportunities that God has placed before you? Hopefully so. But if you're like too many women, you may have fallen into a trap—the trap of taking yourself and your opportunities for granted.

God created you with a surprising array of talents, and He placed you precisely where you are—at a time and place of His choosing. God has done His part by giving you life, love, blessings, and more opportunities than you can count. Your particular situation is unique and so are your opportunities for service and the rest is up to you.

*The Creator has made us each one of a kind. There
is nobody else exactly like us, and there never will be.
Each of us is His special creation
and is alive for a distinctive purpose.*
Luci Swindoll

Love That Forgives

The wisdom that comes from heaven is first of all pure;
then peace-loving, considerate, submissive,
full of mercy and good fruit, impartial and sincere.
James 3:17 NIV

Genuine love is an exercise in forgiveness. If we wish to build lasting relationships, we must learn how to forgive. Why? Because our loved ones are imperfect (as are we). How often must we forgive our family and friends? More times than we can count. Why? Because it's the right thing to do, and it's what God wants us to do.

Perhaps granting forgiveness is hard for you. If so, you're not alone. Genuine, lasting forgiveness is often difficult to achieve. Difficult, but not impossible. Thankfully, with God's help, all things are possible, and that includes forgiveness. But make no mistake: forgiveness is work, which is OK with God. He knows the payoffs are worth the effort.

Perhaps all peacemaking must begin in a similar spot—
in prayer to God, praying for another, asking blessing
for the one who has injured us, and opening
our own hearts for godly examination.
Debra Evans

Disciplining Yourself

Discipline yourself for the purpose of godliness.
1 Timothy 4:7 NASB

Are you a self-disciplined person? If so, congratulations ... if not, maybe it's time to think about your values, your priorities, and your habits. When you pause to consider how much work needs to be done, you'll realize that self-discipline is not simply a proven way to get ahead, it's also an integral element of a well-lived life.

If you seek to maximize your God-given talents, you should adopt a disciplined approach to life. Otherwise, your talents may go unused and your resources may be squandered.

As you plan for your future, remember that life's greatest rewards are unlikely to fall into your lap. On the contrary, your greatest accomplishments will probably require lots of work and plenty of self-discipline. It's up to you.

*It doesn't matter what you are trying to accomplish.
It's all a matter of discipline.*
Wilma Rudolph

June

Hugs for Teammates

A word fitly spoken is like
apples of gold in settings of silver.
Proverbs 25:11 NKJV

L ife is a team sport, and all of us need occasional hugs from our teammates. This world can be a difficult place, a place where many of our friends and family members are troubled by the challenges of everyday life. And since we cannot always be certain who needs our help, we should strive to speak helpful words to all those who cross our paths.

Playwright Alice Childress said, "Life is a short walk from the cradle to the grave, and it behooves us to be kind to one another along the way." How true. Life is far too brief for bitterness, apathy, or animosity.

So make time for the people who need your love and encouragement. They need you, and whether you know it or not, you need them.

My special friends, who know me so well
and love me anyway, give me
daily encouragement to keep on.
Emilie Barnes

On Guard against Evil

Be self-controlled and alert. Your enemy the devil prowls around like a roaring lion looking for someone to devour. Resist him, standing firm in the faith.
1 Peter 5:8–9 NIV

This world is God's creation, and it contains wonderful evidence of His handiwork. But the world also contains countless opportunities to stray from the straight and narrow path that leads to happiness, fulfillment, and health. Temptations are everywhere, and the devil, it seems, never takes a day off. Our task, as thoughtful women living in a dangerous age, is to turn away from temptation and, if need be, to run in the opposite direction.

Evil remains abroad in the world, and far too many people still insist on sowing the seeds of destruction far and wide. We must be on guard against harmful people, harmful habits, and harmful thoughts. And once we've protected ourselves, we should do whatever we can to help our loved ones do the same.

The sad truth is that most evil is done by people who never make up their minds to be either good or evil.
Hannah Arendt

The Power of Faith

*Whatever is born of God overcomes the world.
And this is the victory that has
overcome the world—our faith.*
1 John 5:4 NKJV

Life is a grand adventure made great by faith.
Enduring faith is first experienced at a mother's
knee. There a child learns to trust not only in the
parent but also in the world.

Helen Keller observed, "Faith is a spiritual spotlight that illuminates the path."

And actress Helen Hayes said, "I have doubted;
I have wandered off the path; I have been lost. But I
have always returned; my faith has wavered but has
saved me."

If you're looking for a way to encourage the
world, share your faith in the future, faith in others,
and your faith in the hand that shapes eternity, the
most important faith of all.

*Kill the snake of doubt in your soul,
crush the worms of fear in your heart,
and mountains will move out of your way.*
Kate Seredy

Beyond Fear

*God has not given us a spirit of fear and timidity,
but of power, love, and self-discipline.*
2 Timothy 1:7 NLT

Even the strongest woman may find her courage tested by the inevitable disappointments and tragedies of life. After all, we live in a world filled with uncertainty, hardship, sickness, and danger. Trouble, it seems, is never far from our doorstep.

When we focus on our fears and our doubts, we may find many reasons to lie awake at night and fret about the uncertainties of the coming day. A better strategy is to focus not on our fears but on our opportunities, our abilities, and our God.

So don't dwell on the fears of the day. Instead, trust God's plan and His eternal love for you. And remember: whatever the size of your challenge, God is bigger.

*How very little can be done
under the atmosphere of fear.*
Florence Nightingale

Family Matters

Unless the LORD builds the house,
they labor in vain who build it.
Psalm 127:1 NKJV

Abigail Adams was the first First Lady whose son also became president. The second is Barbara Bush, wife of former President George Herbert Walker Bush and mother of George W. Bush.

With such an impressive clan, it's no surprise that Mrs. Bush had more than a few things to say about family life. Her recommendation was straightforward; she said, "Whatever the times, one thing will never change: if you have children, they must come first. Your success as a family and our success as a society depends not on what happens in the White House, but on what happens inside your house." That's powerful advice from a former First Lady, a First Grandmother, and a first-class mom.

Family life! The United Nations is child's play
compared to the tugs and splits and need to
understand and to forgive that are found in any family.
May Sarton

Perfect Wisdom

The fear of the LORD is the beginning of wisdom,
and knowledge of the Holy one is understanding.
Proverbs 9:10 NIV

The world has its own brand of wisdom, a kind that's often wrong and sometimes dangerous. God, on the other hand, has a different brand of wisdom—a wisdom that will never lead you astray. Where will you place your trust today? Will you trust in the wisdom of fallible men and women, or will you place your faith in God's perfect wisdom? The answer to this question will determine the direction of your day and the quality of your decisions.

Are you tired? Discouraged? Fearful? Be comforted and trust God. Are you worried or anxious? Be confident in God's power. Are you confused? Listen to the quiet voice of your heavenly Father—He is not a God of confusion. Talk with Him; listen to Him; trust Him. His wisdom, unlike the "wisdom" of the world, will never let you down.

Our first step toward gaining God's wisdom is
to know what we do not know;
that is, to be aware of our shortcomings.
Dianna Booher

Using Your Gifts

Do not neglect the spiritual gift within you.
1 Timothy 4:14 NASB

Your talents, resources, and opportunities are gifts from the Giver of all things good. And the best way to say thank you for these gifts is to use them.

Do you have a particular talent? Hone that skill and use it. Do you possess financial resources? Share them. Have you been blessed by a particular opportunity, or have you experienced unusual good fortune? Use it to help others.

When you share the gifts God has given you—especially when you share them freely and without fanfare—you invite God to bless you more and more. So today, do yourself and the world a favor: be a faithful steward of your talents and treasures. Then prepare yourself for even greater blessings that are sure to come.

As simple as it sounds, we all must try to be
the best person we can: by making the best choices,
by making the most of the talents we've been given.
Mary Lou Retton

Looking Fear in the Face

Be on guard. Stand true to what you believe.
Be courageous. Be strong.
1 Corinthians 16:13 NLT

Life can be difficult and discouraging at times. But during our darkest moments, we can depend on our friends and family and on God. When we do, we find the courage to face even the darkest days with hopeful hearts and willing hands.

Eleanor Roosevelt advised, "You gain strength, courage, and confidence by every great experience in which you really stop to look fear in the face. You are able to say to yourself, 'I lived through this horror. I can take the next thing that comes along.' You must do the thing you think you cannot do."

The next time you find your courage tested to the limit, remember that you're probably stronger than you think. And remember—with you, your friends, your family and your God all working together, you have nothing to fear.

Courage doesn't always roar. Sometimes courage
is that little voice at the end of the day that says:
I'll try again tomorrow.
Anne Hunninghake

Destiny's Child

The LORD is good and does what is right;
he shows the proper path.
Psalm 25:8 NLT

At age eighteen Clara Fowler performed on an Oklahoma radio show sponsored by the Page Milk Company. In honor of her sponsor, Clara changed her stage name to Patti Page and began a singing career that led to fifteen gold records. Her biggest hit came in 1951 when she recorded "The Tennessee Waltz," a ballad that was the number one song in America for three solid months.

Looking back on her career, Patti said, "I really do believe in fate, and I think that there was something planned for me to do." The same can be said for you.

If you haven't yet discovered your own life's work, it's not too late to take a page from Patti's book. Keep searching for the role you're destined to play in God's grand plan. When you find it, you'll be a star, wherever you happen to shine.

To keep our faces toward change and
behave like free spirits in the presence of
fate is strength undefeatable.
Helen Keller

Trust in a Good Tomorrow

Blessed is he who trusts in the LORD.
Proverbs 16:20 NIV

Sometimes the future seems bright, and sometimes it does not. Yet even when we can't see the possibilities of tomorrow, God can. Our challenge is to trust God to do the best for us, in spite of our failures.

When we trust God, we should trust Him without reservation. We should steel ourselves against the inevitable disappointments of the day, secure in the knowledge that our heavenly Father has a plan for the future that is brighter than we can imagine.

Are you willing to look to the future with trust and confidence? Hopefully so, because the future should not to be feared; it should be embraced.

When once we are assured that God is good, then there can be nothing left to fear.
Hannah Whitall Smith

The Rule That Is Golden

This royal law is found in the Scriptures:
"Love your neighbor as you love yourself."
If you obey this law, then you are doing right.
James 2:8 ICB

Life is simply better when we treat other people the way we would want to be treated if we were in their shoes. Things go better when we're courteous and compassionate. Graciousness, humility, and kindness are all virtues we should strive for. But sometimes we fall short. Sometimes, amid the busyness and confusion of everyday life, we neglect to share a kind word or a kind deed. This oversight hurts others, but it hurts us as well.

Slow yourself down today, and be alert for those who need your smile, your kind words, your hug, or your helping hand. Make kindness a centerpiece of your dealings with others. They will be blessed, and you will be too.

Believe, when you are most unhappy, that there is something for you to do in the world. So long as you can sweeten another's pain, life is not in vain.
Helen Keller

In Search of Joy

*These things I speak in the world, that they
may have My joy fulfilled in themselves.*
John 17:13 NKJV

Barbara Johnson said, "You have to look for the
joy. Look for the light of God that is hitting your
life, and you will find sparkles you didn't know were
there."

Have you experienced that kind of joy? It's
not enough to hear someone else talk about being
joyful—you must actually experience that kind of
joy in order to understand it.

Should you expect to be a joy-filled woman
twenty-four hours a day, seven days a week, from
this moment on? No. But you can (and should)
experience pockets of joy frequently—that's the
kind of life God offers a woman like you to live.

*Claim the joy that is yours. Pray.
And know that your joy is used
by God to reach others.*
Kay Arthur

Hugs of Kindness

Love is patient; love is kind.
1 Corinthians 13:4 HCSB

It's another stressful day, and you're busily engaged in life. Perhaps a little too busily engaged. So you don't have time to slow down and give anyone a hug, right? Wrong! Even amid the stressful moments of your demanding days, it's important to calm yourself down long enough to sow seeds of kindness. When you do, people will notice.

When you are generous with your time and your praise; when you're quick to share a thoughtful word, a genuine smile, or a helping hand; you demonstrate the power of compassion.

The great humanitarian Albert Schweitzer said, "The purpose of human life is to serve and to show compassion and the will to help others." His words still ring true. Let them ring loudly in your heart.

Love is a multiplication.
Marjory Stoneman Douglas

June 14

Working and Winning

*May the Lord our God show us
his approval and make our efforts successful.
Yes, make our efforts successful!*
Psalm 90:17 NLT

She's coached more championships than anyone else in women's college basketball. Back home in Tennessee, she's more than a successful coach; she's considered a state treasure. Her name is Pat Summitt, and her formula for success is surprisingly simple: "My most valuable secret is that there is no great intangible secret quality to success. It's not touch or talent or a knack. More than anything else, success is simply a matter of consistent hard work."

If you'd like to become a champion, whatever your game, remember that there's a direct correlation between working and winning, on the court and off. As Pat has found, it's the extra effort that will, in time, make your success a slam dunk.

Without discipline, there's no life at all.
Katharine Hepburn

New Beginnings

I will give you a new heart and put a new spirit in you.
Ezekiel 36:26 NIV

If we sincerely want to change ourselves for the better, we must start on the inside and work our way out from there. Lasting change doesn't occur "out there"; it occurs "in here." It occurs, not in the shifting sands of our own particular circumstances, but in the quiet depths of our own hearts.

Are you in search of a new beginning or even a new you? Are you hoping to make dramatic improvements or to break unhealthy habits? If so, don't expect changing circumstances to miraculously transform you into the person you want to become. Transformation starts with God, and it starts in the silent center of a humble human heart—like yours.

When we focus on God, the scene changes.
He's in control of our lives; nothing lies outside
the realm of His redemptive grace. Even when we
make mistakes, fail in relationships, or deliberately
make bad choices, God can redeem us.

Penelope J. Stokes

Peace amid the Chaos

*Depend on the LORD and his strength; always go to
him for help. Remember the miracles he has done;
remember his wonders and his decisions.*
Psalm 105:4–5 NCV

Sometimes peace can be a scarce commodity in
a demanding twenty-first-century world. How,
then, can we find the peace we so desperately desire?
By slowing down, by keeping problems in perspective,
by counting our blessings, and by trusting God.

Dorothy Harrison Pentecost wrote, "Peace is full
confidence that God is who He says He is and that
He will keep every promise in His Word." Fellow
author Beth Moore said, "Prayer guards hearts and
minds and causes God to bring peace out of chaos."

Today, as you journey out into the chaos
of the world, bring God's peace with you. And
remember: the chaos is temporary, but God's peace
is permanent.

*To know God as He really is—in His essential nature
and character—is to arrive at a citadel of peace that
circumstances may storm, but can never capture.*
Catherine Marshall

The Power of Praise

*Praise the LORD! Oh, give thanks to the LORD,
for He is good! For His mercy endures forever.*
Psalm 106:1 NKJV

The book of Psalms has been called the most widely used book of the Old Testament. In the Hebrew version of the Old Testament, the title of the book is translated "Hymns of Praise," and with good reason. Much of the book is a breathtakingly beautiful celebration of God's power, God's love, and God's creation.

One psalmist wrote, "Let everything that has breath praise the LORD. Praise the LORD" (150:6 NIV). Today as you travel to work or school, as you hug your child or kiss your husband, as you gaze at a passing cloud or marvel at a glorious sunset, think of what God has done for you and yours. Every time you notice a gift from the Giver of all things good, praise Him. His works are marvelous, His gifts are beyond understanding, and His love endures forever.

*God is worthy of our praise and is pleased
when we come before Him with thanksgiving.*
Shirley Dobson

Take Care of Yourself

You're addicted to thrills? What an empty life!
The pursuit of pleasure is never satisfied.
Proverbs 21:17 MSG

We live in a world that can be a dangerous place, especially for those who are inclined toward risky behavior. Some risk takers are easy to spot: they jump out of airplanes, scurry up mountains, or race automobiles.

Most risk takers, however, are not so bold. They take more subtle risks that endanger themselves, their friends, and their families. They drink and drive, or they smoke cigarettes, or they neglect to fasten their seat belts, or they engage in countless other behaviors that, while not as glamorous as mountain climbing, are just as dangerous.

This world holds enough hazards without our adding to them by foolishly neglecting our personal safety and the safety of those around us. So the next time you're tempted to do something like that, remember that the body you're putting at risk belongs not only to you but also to God. He and those who love you hope you'll take care of it!

Safety is not a device; it's a state of mind.
Author Unknown

June 19

Living in an Anxious World

GOD *is striding ahead of you. He's right there with you.*
He won't let you down; he won't leave you.
Don't be intimidated. Don't worry.
Deuteronomy 31:8 MSG

We live in a world that often breeds anxiety and fear. When we come face to face with tough times, we may fall prey to discouragement, doubt, or depression. But our Father in heaven has better plans for us. God has promised that we can lead lives of abundance, not anxiety. And we can depend on that promise.

As you face the challenges of daily living, do you find yourself becoming anxious, troubled, discouraged, or fearful? If so, turn every one of your concerns over to your heavenly Father. The same God who created the universe will comfort you if you ask Him. So ask Him—and trust Him. Then watch in amazement as your anxieties melt into the warmth of His loving embrace.

Surely the consolation prize of old age is finding out
how few things are worth worrying over.
Dorothy Dix

Embracing His Promises

Our help is in the name of the Lord,
the Maker of heaven and earth.
Psalm 124:8 HCSB

God has made quite a few promises to you, and He will keep every single one of them.

Author Elisabeth Elliot observed, "We have ample evidence that the Lord is able to guide. The promises cover every imaginable situation. All we need to do is to take the hand He stretches out."

Are you facing a difficult decision? Pause for a moment and have a quiet consultation with your Advisor. Are you fearful, anxious, fretful, or troubled? Slow down long enough to consider God's promises. Those promises never fail, and they never grow old. You can trust them, and you can share them with your family, with your friends, and with the world—starting now and ending never.

Shake the dust from your past,
and move forward in His promises.
Kay Arthur

Honest Work

> *The one who plants and the one who waters*
> *have the same purpose, and each will be*
> *rewarded for his own work.*
> 1 Corinthians 3:8 NCV

An incredibly powerful voice made one preacher's daughter from Detroit a musical icon. A poll even named her the greatest female artist in rock-'n'-roll history. She's Aretha Franklin, a down-to-earth star who attributed much of her success to the honest approach she brings to her craft. She said, "Great work and great music are the result of creative honesty."

A great performance is an honest performance. Today as you step up on your stage, whether at work, home, or school, remember Aretha's success formula—do your work honestly, creatively, and diligently. When you do, your audience will smile—and so will you.

> *Luck? I don't know anything about luck.*
> *I've never banked on it and I'm afraid of*
> *people who do. Luck to me is something else:*
> *hard work—and realizing what is*
> *opportunity and what isn't.*
> Lucille Ball

Beyond Our Regrets

*May the God of hope fill you with all joy
and peace as you trust in him.*
Romans 15:13 NIV

Bitterness can destroy you if you let it—so don't let it!

If you're caught up in intense feelings of anger or regret, you know all too well the destructive power of these emotions. How can you rid yourself of them? First, prayerfully ask God to free you from these feelings. Then you must learn to catch yourself whenever thoughts of bitterness begin to creep up on you. Your challenge is this: to resist negative thoughts before they hijack your emotions.

Poet Christina Rossetti had this sound advice: "Better by far you should forget and smile than you should remember and be sad." It's better to forget than regret.

*Life appears to me too short to be spent
in nursing animosity or registering wrong.*
Charlotte Brontë

Blessings from Above

The Lord is my strength and my song;
He has become my salvation.
Exodus 15:2 HCSB

Sometimes life here on earth can be complicated, demanding, and busy. When the demands of life leave us rushing from place to place with scarcely a moment to spare, we may fail to pause and say a word of thanks for all the good things we've received. But when we fail to count our blessings, we rob ourselves of the happiness, the peace, and the gratitude that should rightfully be ours.

Today, even if you're busily engaged in life, slow down long enough to start counting your blessings. You won't be able to count them all, but take a few moments to jot down as many as you can. Then give thanks to the Giver of all good things: God. His love for you is eternal, and His gifts are plentiful. It's never too soon—or too late—to offer Him thanks.

So much has been given me, I have no time
to ponder over that which has been denied.
Helen Keller

A Prayer for Our Children

I assure you: Whoever does not welcome the kingdom of God like a little child will never enter it.
Luke 18:17 HCSB

Our children are our most precious earthly resource. As responsible adults we must create homes and a homeland in which the next generation can live in safety and in freedom.

Our youngsters have hopes and dreams—most of our children are, by nature, optimists. And it's our responsibility to ensure that they remain optimistic. How can we do that? By creating secure environments in which our children can mature into thoughtful, confident adults.

We inhabit a world that can be a confusing and fearful place. It's a world filled with pressures, temptations, and distractions that pose grave threats to our young people. Today let's make certain we do the important work of caring for our children—all of our children. No work is more important.

Every child born into the world is a new thought of God, an ever-fresh and radiant possibility.
Kate Douglas Wiggin

Where You Belong

*Show family affection to one another with
brotherly love. Outdo one another in showing honor.*
Romans 12:10 HCSB

Dolly Parton was raised in a two-room shack with eleven brothers and sisters in the tiny East Tennessee hamlet of Locust Ridge. Dolly grew up to become one of the most talented and successful country-music performers of all time, but she never forgot her roots, especially her family. After the death of her father, she observed, "I never knew how much I was a daddy's girl until my daddy was gone."

If you're lucky enough to have a loving, caring, family, make your affections known early and often. After all, this earthly circle doesn't remain unbroken forever. The best time to tell loved ones that you love them is now.

*The family: We are a strange little band of characters
trudging through life sharing diseases, toothpaste,
coveting one another's desserts, hiding shampoo,
borrowing money, locking each other out of rooms,
loving, laughing, defending, and trying to figure out
the common thread that bound us all together.*
Erma Bombeck

The Miracles That Await

*Ah Lord GOD! Behold, You have made the heavens
and the earth by Your great power and by
Your outstretched arm! Nothing is too difficult for You.*
Jeremiah 32:17 NASB

When, at the age of two, Helen Keller was stricken with what nineteenth-century doctors called "brain fever," she was left deaf and blind. Helen might have been excused for having a sour attitude about life, but she did not give in to the paralysis of bitterness and despair. Instead, with the help of an extraordinary teacher, young Helen learned to communicate and quickly embraced education.

Eventually, Helen graduated cum laude from Radcliffe College and went on to become a noted American writer and lecturer. She once observed, "When we do the best we can, we never know what miracles await."

What miracles await you? Big ones! When you do your part, God will do His part, and the results will be miraculous!

*Opportunity knocks, but it does not
wake up the person who is asleep.*
Old Saying

Abundant Living

Take heed and beware of covetousness,
for one's life does not consist in
the abundance of the things he possesses.
Luke 12:15 NKJV

She never had an art lesson in her life, but at the age of seventy-six, Anna Mary Robertson, also known as Grandma Moses, took up painting. A busy woman throughout adulthood, she embroidered wool pictures on canvas as a hobby. But when her fingers became too stiff to handle a needle, Anna didn't quit—she just began painting. Her colorful country scenes now hang in museums all over the world.

Grandma Moses once said, "Life is what we make it. Always has been. Always will be." She backed up her words with actions. So should we.

You, like Anna Mary Robertson, are a woman with the opportunity to fully engage in life. Seize that opportunity today—and keep seizing it every day you live.

Live your life while you have it.
Life is a splendid gift.
There is nothing small about it.
Florence Nightingale

Asking and Receiving

Ask and it will be given to you; seek and you will find.
Luke 11:9 NIV

Sometimes, amid the demands and the frustrations of daily life, we forget to slow down long enough to talk with God. Instead of turning our thoughts and prayers to Him, we rely entirely on our own resources, with decidedly mixed results. Or, instead of praying for strength, we seek to manufacture it within ourselves, only to find that lasting strength remains elusive.

Are you in need? Ask God to sustain you. And while you're making requests, don't be afraid to ask for the loving support of your family and friends. When you ask for help, you're likely to receive it. But if you're unwilling to ask, why should you expect to receive any?

When the going gets tough, remember that help is on the way. All you have to do is ask.

God will help us become the people we are meant to be, if only we will ask Him.
Hannah Whitall Smith

During the Darkest Days

I have heard your prayer; I have seen your tears.
Look, I will heal you.
2 Kings 20:5 HCSB

The sadness that accompanies any significant loss is an inevitable part of life. In time sadness runs its course and gradually abates. Depression, on the other hand, is a physical and emotional condition that is, in almost all cases, treatable with medication and counseling.

Some days are light and happy, and some days are not. When we face the dark days of life, we must choose how we will respond. We bring light to those dark days by turning first to God and then to trusted family members, friends, and medical professionals. When we do, the clouds will eventually part, and the sun will shine once more in our souls.

Concern should drive us into action
and not into depression.
Karen Horney

Encouragement Is Contagious

> *Bright eyes cheer the heart;*
> *good news strengthens the bones.*
> Proverbs 15:30 HCSB

A woman's attitude is contagious. If she is optimistic and upbeat, her family will tend to feel similar emotions. But if a mother or sister or daughter falls prey to pessimism and doubt, the family suffers right along with her.

Wise women like you understand the power of encouragement. Marie T. Freeman said, "Encouragement starts at home, but it should never end there."

And Nicole Johnson observed, "Encouragement is to a friendship what confetti is to a party."

So if you'd like to make your corner of the world a happier, healthier place, spread encouragement wherever you go. You'll be amazed at how fast it can spread.

> *If someone listens or stretches out a hand or*
> *whispers a word of encouragement or*
> *attempts to understand a lonely person,*
> *extraordinary things begin to happen.*
> Loretta Girzartis

July

Daily Blessings

Bless the LORD, O my soul,
and forget not all his benefits.
Psalm 103:2 KJV

If you're like most women, you're very busy. Your life is probably hectic, demanding, and complicated. When the demands of life leave you scurrying around with scarcely a free moment, it's easy to forget to thank God for the blessings He has bestowed.

But no matter how busy you are, you should never be too busy to thank God for His gifts. Then, with gratitude in your heart, you can face your daily duties with the perspective and power that only He can provide.

As you plan for the day ahead, include plans to thank God for all His blessings. You owe your heavenly Father so many things, including your praise.

Each day comes bearing its own gifts.
Untie the ribbons.
Ruth Ann Schabacker

When You Set Your Mind

Well-done work has its own reward.
Proverbs 12:14 MSG

South Florida native Chris Evert won Wimbledon three times, the Australian Open twice, and the French Open seven times on the way to eighteen Grand Slam singles titles. When questioned about her success, she said, "You can do almost anything you set your mind to, if you're willing to work hard enough. With hard work, the world is your oyster."

If you haven't yet cracked your oyster, consider the tennis champ's words and get busy. When you combine a little natural talent with a lot of elbow grease, amazing things can happen. And if you're willing to pay that price, it's point, set, match, and you win!

Help yourself and God will help you.
Joan of Arc

Hugs for the Family

Above all, love each other deeply,
because love covers over a multitude of sins.
1 Peter 4:8 NIV

In this fast-paced world, life can be difficult and pressures intense. As those pressures build, you may tend to focus so intently on your obligations that you lose sight, however temporarily, of your spiritual and emotional needs. (That's one reason a regular daily quiet time is so important—it offers a badly needed dose of perspective.)

Even when the demands of life are great, never forget that you have been entrusted with a profound responsibility: the responsibility of contributing to your family's emotional and spiritual well-being. It's a big job, but with God's help, you're up to the task. Let the hugs begin!

Call it a clan, call it a network, call it a tribe,
call it a family. Whatever you call it,
whoever you are, you need it.
Jane Howard

The Wisdom of Moderation

*Take heed to yourselves, lest your hearts be
weighed down with carousing,
drunkenness, and cares of this life.*
Luke 21:34 NKJV

Moderation and wisdom are traveling companions. If we're wise, we'll learn to temper our
appetites, our desires, and our impulses. When we
do, we'll be blessed—in part because God has created a world in which temperance is rewarded and
intemperance is inevitably punished.

Would you like to improve your life? Then harness your appetites and restrain your impulses. Moderation is difficult, especially in a prosperous society
such as ours. But the rewards of moderation are numerous and long lasting.

No one can force you to control your appetites.
The decision to live temperately is yours and yours
alone. But you'll do yourself a monumental favor
when you decide wisely.

Perhaps too much of everything is as bad as too little.
Edna Ferber

Gentleness of Spirit

As those who have been chosen of God,
holy and beloved, put on a heart of compassion,
kindness, humility, gentleness and patience.
Colossians 3:12 NASB

Sometimes it's difficult to be gentle. As fallible human beings, we're subject to the normal frustrations of daily life, and when we become frustrated, we're tempted to strike out in anger. But as Marie T. Freeman observed, "When you strike out in anger, you strike out!"

As long as you live, you will face countless opportunities to lose your temper over small, relatively insignificant events: a traffic jam, a spilled cup of coffee, an inconsiderate comment, a broken promise. When you're tempted to lose your temper over these inconveniences, don't. Turn away from anger and turn instead to God; when you do, He will fill you with a loving spirit that will help you deal gently and generously with others.

Nothing is as strong as gentleness,
nothing so gentle as real strength.
Saint Francis de Sales

Unbending Truth

Job continued his discourse . . .
I will never admit you are in the right;
till I die, I will not deny my integrity.
Job 27:1, 5 NIV

Author Beth Moore correctly observed, "Those who walk in truth walk in liberty." We must seek to live each day with discipline, honesty, and faith. When we do, at least two things happen: integrity becomes a habit, and God finds ways to reward us for our obedience to Him.

Living a life of integrity isn't always the easiest way, but it's always the right way. And God clearly intends that it should be our way.

Character isn't built overnight; it is built slowly over a lifetime. It is the sum of every sensible choice, every honorable decision, and every honest word. It is forged on the anvil of sincerity and polished by the virtue of fairness. Character is a precious thing—preserve yours at all costs.

Character is what we are in the dark.
Old Saying

Carrying the Load

God blesses the people who patiently endure testing.
Afterward they will receive the crown of life
that God has promised to those who love him.
James 1:12 NLT

In the 1940s, actresses of African-American descent were relegated to bit parts. The movies, it seemed, weren't ready for someone like Lena Horne. But Lena was ready for them. She parlayed a ton of talent and beauty into a career as a leading lady, unheard of in those days for a woman of color. In looking back on her career, Lena was philosophical. She said, "The size of your burden is never as important as the way you carry it."

The next time you face a heavy burden, remember that there is a good way and a bad way to carry every load. The best way is to keep working, keep believing, and never give in to discouragement. Because, as Lena Horne correctly observed, no load is too heavy if you discover the right way to carry it—but no load is light if you don't.

Trouble is a tunnel through which we pass and not
a brick wall against which we must break our heads.
Claire Weeks

Hugs for Those Who May (or May Not) Deserve Them

Love your enemies. Pray for those who hurt you.
Matthew 5:44 ICB

Sometimes people deserve hugs, and sometimes they don't. When folks are behaving well, it's easy to love them and easy to hug them. But when they misbehave, it's hard to hug and even harder to forgive.

Yet when we fail to forgive those who have hurt us, we hurt ourselves. As centenarian and author Marie T. Freeman said, "Bitterness is the price we charge ourselves for being unwilling to forgive."

But holocaust survivor Corrie ten Boom knew, "Forgiveness is the key which unlocks the door of resentment and the handcuffs of hatred. It breaks the chains of bitterness and the shackles of selfishness."

So here's something to try: find somebody who doesn't "deserve" a hug today, and hug that person anyway. You'll discover that forgiveness and happiness go hand in hand.

Forgiveness does not mean the perpetrator goes free; it means that the forgiver is free and that God will justly deal with those who have caused pain.
Cynthia Heald

Practicing What We Preach

When people do not accept divine guidance,
they run wild. But whoever obeys the law is happy.
Proverbs 29:18 NLT

A re you willing to practice the philosophies you preach? Hopefully so; otherwise, you'll be tormented by inconsistencies between your beliefs and your behaviors. If you'd like to enjoy the rewards of a clear conscience, it's up to you (and only you) to make certain your actions are guided by your beliefs.

Nobel Peace Prize winner Jane Addams once noted, "The worth of every conviction consists precisely in the steadfastness with which it is held." How steadfastly do you hold your convictions? If your convictions are firmly held and clearly demonstrated by your actions, congratulations! You've already learned one of life's most important lessons: convictions aren't really worth very much until they're put into practice.

When your good behavior speaks
for itself . . . don't interrupt.
Author Unknown

Let's Get Organized!

*God hasn't invited us into a disorderly, unkempt life
but into something holy and beautiful—
as beautiful on the inside as the outside.*
1 Thessalonians 4:7 MSG

If there is a secret to effective work, it's organization;
too much clutter makes effective work impossible.
The greater the amount of disorder in your life, the
greater will be the difficulties in accomplishing your
goals. But when you introduce organization into
your daily affairs, you'll begin reaping surprising
dividends.

No one can organize your life but you. It's up
to you to invest the time and energy required to
arrange your workplace and your home in an orderly
fashion. So clean out that closet. Clear off that desk.
Handle a piece of paper one time and be done with
it. Keep an accurate daily calendar and stick by your
appointments. And remember: if you're looking for
a surefire way to clean up your life, clean out the
clutter. Organization is good for the soul.

*Whenever I meet people who tell me they are stuck,
I know that if I visit their homes,
I will almost always find lots of clutter.
Clutter accumulates when energy stagnates.*
Karen Kingston

Happiness for Today

Delight thyself also in the LORD;
and he shall give thee the desires of thine heart.
Psalm 37:4 KJV

After graduating from Barnard College in 1928, this anthropologist wrote about American folklore. She became the most widely read black woman in America but was later abandoned by the publishing world. She died, largely forgotten, and was buried in an unmarked grave. Thankfully, however, the works of Zora Neale Hurston were rediscovered and are once again in print and widely enjoyed.

Zora once observed, "Happiness is nothing but everyday living seen through a veil." If you'd like to squeeze a little more enjoyment out of your day, don't look far out on the horizon. Your happiness, as this celebrated author knew, is woven into the fabric of everyday living. And if you don't find happiness close to home, you're unlikely to find it anywhere else.

Life is like a butterfly. You can chase it,
or you can let it come to you.
Ruth Brown

Eying the Doughnut

This hope we have as an anchor of the soul,
a hope both sure and steadfast.
Hebrews 6:19 NASB

On the wall of a little doughnut shop, the sign read: "As you travel through life, brother, whatever be your goal, keep your eye upon the doughnut, and not upon the hole."

Are you a woman who keeps your eye upon the doughnut, or have you acquired the unfortunate habit of looking only at the hole? Hopefully, you spend most of your waking hours thanking God for the good things in life and ignoring the rest.

Today and every day do yourself this favor: choose to be a hope-filled, upbeat, enthusiastic woman. Think optimistically about your life and your future. Trust your hopes, not your fears. Whatever you do, keep your eye carefully fixed on the doughnut and don't waste too much time fretting about that silly little hole.

No pessimist ever discovered the secrets of the stars,
or sailed to an unchartered land,
or opened a new heaven to the human spirit.
Helen Keller

Knowledge and Wisdom

*It is not good to have zeal without knowledge,
nor to be hasty and miss the way.*
Proverbs 19:2 NIV

To grow as a woman, you need both knowledge and wisdom. Knowledge is found in textbooks. Wisdom, on the other hand, is obtained through experience, years of trial and error, and careful attention to God's Word. Knowledge is an important building block in a well-lived life, and it pays rich dividends both personally and professionally. But wisdom is even more important because it refashions not only our minds but also our hearts.

When it comes to your faith, God doesn't intend for you to stand still. He wants you to keep growing as a woman and as a spiritual being. No matter how grown-up you may be, you still have more growing to do. And the more you grow, the more beautiful you become, inside and out.

*Let us remember that the longer we live,
the more we know, and the more we know,
the more beautiful we are.*
Marianne Williamson

Priorities for Marriage and Family

> Let each one of you in particular so love
> his own wife as himself, and let the wife
> see that she respects her husband.
> Ephesians 5:33 NKJV

It takes time to build strong family ties—lots of time. Yet we live in a world where time seems to be an ever-shrinking commodity.

Has the busy pace of life robbed you of sufficient time with your loved ones? If so, it's time to fine-tune your priorities. Nothing is more important than the time you spend with that little band of men, women, and children who comprise your immediate family.

As the old proverb says, "When the whole family is together, the soul is in place." Make sure the soul of the family is in place at your place.

> You have heard about "quality time" and
> "quantity time." Your family needs both.
> Mary Prince

July 15

An Exercise in Well-Being

*Didn't you realize that your body is a sacred place,
the place of the Holy Spirit? Don't you see that
you can't live however you please, squandering
what God paid such a high price for?*
1 Corinthians 6:19 MSG

A healthy lifestyle includes regular, sensible, physical exercise. How much exercise is right for you? That's a decision you should make in consultation with your physician. But make no mistake: if you sincerely desire to be a thoughtful caretaker of the body God has given you, exercise is vital.

Once you begin a regular exercise program, you'll discover that the benefits are not merely physical but also psychological. Regular exercise helps to clear your head and lift your spirits while building your muscles.

If you've been taking your body for granted, today is a wonderful day to change. When you do, you'll have the peace and pride of knowing you've done your part to protect and preserve the body God has entrusted to your care.

*Mind and body in harmony provide all
the necessary strength for happy, healthy living.*
Charmaine Saunders

Good Pressure, Bad Pressure

He who walks with the wise grows wise,
but a companion of fools suffers harm.
Proverbs 13:20 NIV

Our world is filled with pressures: some good, some bad. The pressures we feel to behave responsibly are positive ones. God places these pressures on our hearts, and He intends that we act according to them. But we also face different pressures, ones that are not from God.

Society seeks to mold us into more worldly beings; God seeks to mold us into new beings, more spiritual beings, beings that are not conformed to this world.

If we desire to lead responsible lives—and if we seek to please God—we must resist the pressures some people seek to impose upon us. We must resist the temptation to do the popular thing—what others think we should do or what other people are doing—and insist instead on doing the right thing. Finding wise friends will help you stay the course.

Be decent and fair. But ultimately you have to
know how to get the work done,
whether or not people like you for it.
Sally Field

When the Answer Is No

Speak, for your servant is listening.
1 Samuel 3:10 NIV

God answers our prayers. What God does not do is this: He does not always answer our prayers as soon as we might like, and He does not always answer our prayers by saying yes.

God isn't an order taker, and He's not some sort of cosmic vending machine. Sometimes—even when we want something very badly—our loving heavenly Father responds to our requests by saying no—and we must accept His answer, even if we don't understand it.

God answers prayers not only according to our wishes but also according to His master plan. We cannot know that plan, but we can know the Planner. And we must trust His wisdom, His righteousness, and His love—always.

Let's never forget that some of God's greatest mercies are His refusals. He says no in order that He may, in some way we cannot imagine, say yes. All His ways with us are merciful. His meaning is always love.
Elisabeth Elliot

A Happy Ending

*We also rejoice in our sufferings, because we know
that suffering produces perseverance;
perseverance, character; and character, hope.*
Romans 5:3–4 NIV

Mary Tyler Moore played Laura on *The Dick Van
Dyke Show* and then starred in her own TV hit,
The Mary Tyler Moore Show. But behind the camera,
life has not always been a string of happy endings
for Ms. Moore. This determined woman has waged
a personal battle with diabetes, experienced the
pain of divorce, and lost a son in a tragic handgun
accident. Yet the beloved actress wisely noted, "Pain
nourishes courage. You can't be brave if you've only
had wonderful things happen to you."

If the story of your life has had a few unhappy
endings, remember that here on earth, adversity
is par for the course. But despite life's occasional
hardships, when it comes to writing your own story,
the ending is up to you.

*Often God shuts a door in our face so that He
can open the door through which He wants us to go.*
Catherine Marshall

God Is Love

*God is love, and the one who remains in love
remains in God, and God remains in him.*
1 John 4:16 HCSB

God is love. It's a sweeping statement, a profoundly important description of what God is and how He works. God's love is perfect. When we open our hearts to His perfect love, we are touched by the Creator's hand, and we are transformed.

Barbara Johnson observed, "We cannot protect ourselves from trouble, but we can dance through the puddles of life with a rainbow smile, twirling the only umbrella we need—the umbrella of God's love."

English mystical writer Juliana of Norwich said, "We are so preciously loved by God that we cannot even comprehend it. No created being can ever know how much and how sweetly and tenderly God loves them."

Today, even if you can only carve out a few quiet moments, offer sincere prayers of thanksgiving to your Father. Thank Him for His blessings and love.

*I am convinced our hearts are not healthy until
they have been satisfied by the only completely healthy
love that exists: the love of God Himself.*
Beth Moore

A Hug for Parents

*Good people who live honest lives
will be a blessing to their children.*
Proverbs 20:7 NCV

We love our parents, but sometimes we may be slow to demonstrate that love. We assume, quite correctly, that our parents know how much we love them—but we may neglect to verbalize our feelings. When we withhold sentiments of love and appreciation from our parents, we do a disservice to them and to ourselves.

Giving our parents the respect (and the hugs) they deserve shows them that we understand and appreciate the countless sacrifices they've made on our behalf. That's why, as faithful, appreciative children, we should be quick to say, "Thanks, Mom and Dad"—and we should say it not only with our words but also with our deeds, with our hugs, and with our prayers.

Parenthood is the world's most intensive course in love.
Polly Berrien Berends

When Mountains Move

He granted their request because they trusted in Him.
1 Chronicles 5:20 HCSB

Are you a woman who confidently asks God to move mountains, or do you timidly ask Him to push around a few molehills? God is perfectly capable of moving either molehills or mountains, so it's up to you to decide whether you want His help on big projects or just on the small ones.

God has promised that when you ask for His help, He will not withhold it. So ask. Ask Him to meet the needs of your day. Ask Him for wisdom. Ask Him to lead you, to protect you, and to correct you. And don't hesitate to ask Him to do big things in your life and in the lives of your loved ones.

God stands at the door and waits. When you knock on His door, He answers. Your task, of course, is to seek His guidance prayerfully, confidently, and often.

God uses our most stumbling,
faltering faith-steps as the open door to
His doing for us "more than we ask or think."
Catherine Marshall

Learning to Say No

*Grow a wise heart—you'll do yourself a favor;
keep a clear head—you'll find a good life.*
Proverbs 19:8 MSG

The greatest time-saving mechanism—and the most underutilized—is the word *no*. Until you learn to say no politely, firmly, and often, you'll find your calendar clogged with time-consuming commitments.

People who overcommit and underserve lead lives filled with endless complications: they find themselves overworked, underappreciated, over-stressed, and underpaid.

You can simplify your life by making a simple yet powerful pledge: promise to undertake only those things you can do and do well. Treat your time as you would treat any other priceless asset, and watch the changes a simple two-letter word can make in your life.

*If you just set out to be liked, you would be
prepared to compromise on anything at any time,
and you would achieve nothing.*
Margaret Thatcher

Blessed beyond Measure

*The LORD bless you and keep you; the LORD make
His face shine upon you, and be gracious to you.*
Numbers 6:24–25 NKJV

As we begin each day, we should pause to consider God's blessings. Even though His gifts to
us are too numerous to count, we should make a
start nonetheless.

The Greek biographer Plutarch said that "the
worship most acceptable to God comes from a
thankful and cheerful heart."

Marianne Williamson, international lecturer
on spiritual, personal, and political issues, also
recognized the importance of counting our blessings.
She said, "Joy is what happens to us when we allow
ourselves to recognize how good things really are."

Today, as a way of saying thanks to the Giver of
all things good, thank God for His gifts, use His gifts
to the best of your ability, and share His gifts with
others. Then God, you, and others will be blessed.

*Come up from the lowlands; there are heights
yet to climb. You cannot do healthful thinking
in the lowlands. Look to the mountaintop for faith.*
Mary McLeod Bethune

Making the Choice to Forgive

Whenever you stand praying, forgive, if you have anything against anyone, so that your Father who is in heaven will also forgive you your transgressions.
Mark 11:25 NASB

Forgiveness is a choice. We can choose to forgive those who have injured us, or we can choose not to. When we follow God's teachings by offering forgiveness to His children, we will be blessed. But when we allow bitterness and resentment to poison our hearts, we suffer from our own shortsightedness.

Do you harbor resentment against anyone? If so, you're faced with an important decision: whether to forgive the person who has hurt you. God's instructions are clear: He wants you to forgive. Period.

To forgive or not to forgive: that is the question. The answer should be obvious. The time to forgive is now . . . always now.

May I forget what ought to be forgotten and recall unfailingly all that ought to be recalled.
Laura Palmer

God Is Here

Fear thou not; for I am with thee.
Isaiah 41:10 KJV

Since God is everywhere, we are free to enjoy His presence whenever we take the time to quiet our souls and turn our prayers toward Him. But sometimes, amid the incessant demands of life, we allow our thoughts to stray far from God. And when we do, we suffer.

Do you schedule a regular meeting each day with the Creator? You should. During these moments of stillness, you will gain direction, perspective, and peace—God's peace. You'll sense the loving presence of your heavenly Father and be comforted by the certain knowledge that God is not far away. He isn't even nearby. He is, quite literally, here.

What a comfort to know that God is present there in your life, available to meet every situation with you, that you are never left to face any problem alone.
Vonette Bright

Your Happy Face

*Strength and dignity are her clothing, and
she smiles at the future. She opens her mouth in
wisdom, and the teaching of kindness is on her tongue.
She looks well to the ways of her household,
and does not eat the bread of idleness.*
Proverbs 31:25–27 NASB

Marilyn Monroe once observed, "I want to grow
old without facelifts; I want to be loyal to the
face I made." Tragically, she never got that chance,
but the rest of us can still learn a lesson from her
words.

The lives we live and the decisions we make
eventually become etched on our faces. As the old
saying goes, wrinkles should be tracks where smiles
have been.

So why not make your face a place where
thousands of smiles leave their traces? When you
do, you'll be secure in the knowledge that you've
done your part to enrich a world that needs every
single smile it can get.

*Smile at each other, smile at your wife, smile at your
husband, smile at your children, smile at each other—
it doesn't matter who it is—and that will help you
to grow up in greater love for each other.*
Mother Teresa

July 27

Financial Wisdom 101

The wise have wealth and luxury,
but fools spend whatever they get.
Proverbs 21:20 NLT

You've probably heard this advice on thousands of occasions: spend less than you make. It sounds easy, but it's hard to spend money wisely. After all, we live in a world that's filled to the brim with wonderful things to buy and wonderful people telling us how much we need to buy those things. But sometimes our desires for more and better stuff can exceed our ability to pay for those things.

The answer to the problem of overspending is straightforward. First we must earn money through honest work for which we are well suited; then we must spend less than we earn (and save or invest the rest intelligently). That's Financial Wisdom 101 . . . class dismissed.

The best money advice I ever got was from my father.
He said, "Don't spend anything unless you have to."
Dinah Shore

July 28

The Problem Solver

People who do what is right may have many problems,
but the LORD will solve them all.
Psalm 34:19 NCV

In 1967 a diving accident left young Joni Eareckson a quadriplegic. But she didn't give up on life. Unable to use her hands, she taught herself to paint fine art by holding a brush between her teeth. Then the determined woman began writing. To date she's completed more than thirty books, and her ministry, Joni and Friends, touches the lives of millions.

The next time you face a difficult day or an unexpected challenge, remember Joni's journey. If she could meet her challenges, you can meet yours with the same courage and determination. Take heart, trust, and remember that no problem is too big for God.

If we had no winter, the spring would not be so
pleasant; if we did not sometimes taste of adversity,
prosperity would not be so welcome.
Anne Bradstreet

The Joys of Friendship

As iron sharpens iron, a friend sharpens a friend.
Proverbs 27:17 NLT

What is a friend? The dictionary defines *friend* as "a person who is attached to another by feelings of affection or personal regard." That's accurate as far as it goes, but when we examine the deeper meaning of friendship, many more descriptors come to mind: trustworthiness, loyalty, helpfulness, kindness, understanding, forgiveness, encouragement, humor, and cheerfulness, to mention but a few. Friends are good for each other. They not only encourage but also challenge and sharpen each other.

Genuine friendship is something to be treasured and nourished. One way we do that is by treating others as we wish to be treated. When we treat others with kindness, courtesy, and respect, we build friendships that can last a lifetime.

Some people come into our lives and quickly go.
Some people stay for a while and leave footprints
on our hearts, and we are never the same.
Author Unknown

Trusting the Shepherd

He maketh me to lie down in green pastures:
he leadeth me beside the still waters.
He restoreth my soul.
Psalm 23:2–3 KJV

When our dreams come true and our plans prove successful, we find it easy to thank God and to trust His divine providence. But in times of sorrow or hardship, we may find ourselves questioning God's plans for our lives.

On occasion you will confront circumstances that trouble you to the very core of your soul. It's during these difficult times that you must find the wisdom and the courage to trust God despite your circumstances.

Are you a woman who seeks God's blessings for yourself and your family? Then trust Him. Trust Him with your relationships. Trust Him with your priorities. Follow His commandments and pray for His guidance—and prepare yourself for the abundance and peace that will most certainly be yours when you trust the Shepherd.

Since the Lord is your shepherd,
what are you worried about?
Marie T. Freeman

Getting It All Done

The LORD will be a refuge for His people.
Joel 3:16 HCSB

All of us have moments when we feel drained. All of us suffer through difficult days, trying times, and perplexing periods in our lives. But God stands ready and willing to give us comfort and strength if we turn to Him.

Burning the candle at both ends is tempting but potentially destructive. Instead, we should learn to say no to the things we simply don't have time or energy to do.

If you're a woman with too many demands and too few hours in which to meet them, don't fret. Focus on God and on His love for you. Take time to prioritize your life, putting first things first. You can summon the energy to do the most important things on today's to-do list, and let go of the others.

Does God care about all the responsibilities
we have to juggle in our daily lives? Of course.
But He cares more that our lives demonstrate balance,
the ability to discern what is essential
and give ourselves fully to it.

Penelope J. Stokes

August

We Are All Role Models

*You should be an example to the believers in speech,
in conduct, in love, in faith, in purity.*
1 Timothy 4:12 HCSB

Whether we like it or not, all of us are role models. Our friends and family members watch our actions and often pattern their responses or even their lives accordingly. As the old saying goes, "Example is a language anyone can read."

What kind of example are you? Are you the kind of woman whose life serves as a genuine example of righteousness? Are you the kind of woman whose actions, day in and day out, are based on kindness, faithfulness, and generosity? If so, you're not only blessed by God, you're also a powerful force for good in a world that desperately needs positive influences such as yours.

*If you want to be respected for your actions,
then your behavior must be above reproach.*
Rosa Parks

All in the Family

*If anyone does not provide for his own, and especially
for those of his household, he has denied the faith.*
1 Timothy 5:8 NASB

As every woman knows, family life is a mixture of conversations, mediations, commiserations, deliberations, frustrations, negotiations, irritations, and celebrations. In other words, the life of a typical mom is incredibly varied.

Author Anne Ortlund said, "Money can build or buy a house. Add love to that and you have a home. Add God to that and you have a temple. You have 'a little colony of the kingdom of heaven.'"

In the life of every family, there are moments of frustration and disappointment. But for those who are lucky enough to be part of a close-knit, caring family circle, the rewards far outweigh the frustrations.

*When you look at your life,
the greatest happiness is family happiness.*
Joyce Brothers

A Dream Come True

Where there is no vision, the people perish.
Proverbs 29:18 KJV

Carol Burnett lived in Los Angeles but dreamed of being a star on Broadway. So she packed her bags, moved to New York, and followed that dream. At first she couldn't find work, but gradually she blossomed, and in 1967 she landed her own TV show. This comedy legend's advice was simple: "When you've got a dream, you've got to grab it and never let go."

If you've got a dream you haven't yet grabbed on to, remember the skinny college kid who moved across a continent to apprehend hers. Then, like the young Carol Burnett, you can do more than dream; you can get busy making your dream a reality. Dreams can and do come true, but they usually need help from you.

It is never too late to dream or to start something new.
Luci Swindoll

Courage and Character

"Have courage, daughter. . . .
Your faith has made you well."
Matthew 9:22 HCSB

Helen Keller could have been speaking about our generation when she offered this piece of wisdom: "Character cannot be developed in ease and quiet. Only through trial and suffering is the soul strengthened."

In this new millennium the world seems filled with enough trials and suffering to last until the next millennium. And in such trying times we may be tempted to take shortcuts. But as famous opera singer Beverly Sills said, "There are no shortcuts to any place worth going." When facing difficult times—whether as a nation or as individuals—what's required is character, and lots of it.

So the next time you come face to face with trouble, don't back down. You can get through the tough times with a good old-fashioned, double-barrel dose of courage and character.

You'll never do a whole lot
unless you're brave enough to try.
Dolly Parton

Today

The LORD is my inheritance;
therefore, I will hope in him!
Lamentations 3:24 NLT

It's sad but true: most of us find it surprisingly easy to take for granted the gift of life. As Austrian writer Marie von Ebner-Eschenbach observed, "Nothing is so often irretrievably missed as a daily opportunity."

Miguel de Cervantes, the Spanish novelist, dramatist, and poet, wrote, "Tomorrow will be a new day. When God sends the dawn, He sends it for all." Four hundred years after those words were penned, they still apply. Each new day is a fresh opportunity for all.

Today you have been given another chance at life. This is a new day, another opportunity to live, to love, to rejoice, and to contribute. Consider this day a gift, a sacred treasure to be savored and shared.

Yesterday is a cancelled check; tomorrow is
a promissory note; today is
the only cash you have—so spend it wisely.
Kay Lyons

Expecting a Terrific Tomorrow

> *Wisdom is pleasing to you. If you find it,*
> *you have hope for the future.*
> Proverbs 24:14 NCV

How bright is your future? The answer, in all likelihood, is that your future is so bright that you'd better wear shades!

Now, here's something else to ponder: how bright do you believe your future to be? Are you expecting a terrific tomorrow, or are you dreading a terrible one? And make no mistake: the answer to this second set of questions will have a powerful impact on the way your tomorrow turns out.

Corrie ten Boom had this advice: "When the train goes through a tunnel and the world becomes dark, do you jump out? Of course not. You sit still and trust the engineer to get you through." Her advice applies to all of us. It's time to trust God . . . and put on the shades.

> *The future lies all before us. Shall it only be a slight*
> *advance upon what we usually do? Ought it not to be*
> *a bound, a leap forward to altitudes of endeavor and*
> *success undreamed of before?*
> Annie Armstrong

Making It Look Easy

> *Do you see any truly competent workers?*
> *They will serve kings rather than ordinary people.*
> Proverbs 22:29 NLT

In 1976 skater Dorothy Hamill won the Olympic figure-skating gold medal in Innsbruck, Austria. The young girl with the signature "wedge" hairstyle went on to become perhaps the most popular and sought-after figure skater of her generation.

Like all great skaters, Dorothy made even the most difficult routines look effortless. She said, "That's what skating is all about: trying to make it look as though it flows."

In skating, as in life, it takes lots of effort to make things look effortless. So if you'd like to give your performance that memorable Dorothy Hamill flair, remember that although sometimes it's hard to make things look easy, for quality-conscious women like you, it's worth it.

> *God's never been guilty of sponsoring a flop.*
> Ethel Waters

Seeking God (and Finding Him)

*The LORD sees every heart and understands
and knows every plan and thought.
If you seek him, you will find him.*
1 Chronicles 28:9 NLT

If we genuinely look for God, we need not look far.
He is with us. Sometimes, however, in the crush of
our daily duties, God may seem far away. Yet God is
everywhere we have ever been and everywhere we
will ever go. He's with us night and day; He knows
our thoughts and our prayers. And when we earnestly
seek Him, we'll find Him because He's here, waiting
patiently for us to reach out to Him.

Elisabeth Elliot said, "It is God to whom and with
whom we travel, while He is the End of our journey,
He is also at every stopping place." No matter our
circumstances, God never leaves us. He's always
right here.

*God is a place of safety you can run to,
but it helps if you are running to Him on a daily basis
so that you are in familiar territory.*
Stormie Omartian

The Search for Happiness

*Lead a tranquil and quiet life
in all godliness and dignity.*
1 Timothy 2:2 HCSB

Happiness depends less on our circumstances than on our thoughts. When we turn our thoughts to things positive—when we thank God for His gifts and revel in His glorious creation, those positive thoughts bring a reward. But when we focus on the negative aspects of life, we invite needless suffering into our own lives and the lives of our loved ones.

The Roman poet Horace noted, "You traverse the world in search of happiness, which is within reach of every person—a contented mind confers it all." Happiness is, to a surprising extent, a creation of our own making.

Here are two facts worth considering: first, happiness is a choice; second, no one can choose your happiness but yourself. Happiness is in your own hands—take it!

*If you have a negative thought, don't waste hours
thinking about it. Simply direct yourself
to something positive and keep repeating the positive
until you eliminate the negative.*
Tina Louise

Freedom from Spiritual Traps

Where the Spirit of the Lord is, there is freedom.
2 Corinthians 3:17 NIV

We frail human beings lose hope from time to time. When we do, we need the encouragement of friends and the life-changing power of prayer.

If we find ourselves falling into the spiritual traps of worry, discouragement, or despair, we can seek direction from God, and we can also solicit the encouraging words of friends and family members. God has promised that peace and joy are ours if we will only take the steps necessary to claim them.

Juliana of Norwich noted, "Peace and love are always alive in us, but we are not always alive to peace and love." Our task, simply put, is to guard ourselves against the spiritual traps that might trip us up and then to claim the peace, the love, and the power that can be ours.

Our body is like armor, our soul
like the warrior. Take care of both,
and you will be ready for what comes.
Amma Syncletica

The Fountain of Youth

Youth may be admired for vigor,
but gray hair gives prestige to old age.
Proverbs 20:29 MSG

She made her debut on a Brooklyn stage in 1901 and performed regularly for the next seventy years. She often played a woman of questionable virtue, but her talent for self-promotion was never in question. Her name was Mae West—the woman who said, "You're never too old to become a little younger." And she was right.

A youthful attitude is the closest thing yet found to the fountain of youth. So if your life is becoming a little too serious, maybe it's time to lighten up, to have a little more fun, and to think a little bit more like a kid. Whether you're seventeen, seventy, or a hundred and seven, you're never too old to think young.

We turn not older with years, but newer every day.
Emily Dickinson

The Beauty That Surrounds Us

> *God's glory is on tour in the skies,*
> *God-craft on exhibit across the horizon.*
> Psalm 19:1 MSG

Each morning the sun rises upon a glorious world that is a physical manifestation of God's infinite power and His infinite love. And yet we're sometimes too busy to notice.

We live in a society filled with more distractions than we can possibly count and more obligations than we can possibly meet. Is it any wonder, then, that we often overlook God's handiwork as we rush from place to place, giving scarcely a single thought to the beauty that surrounds us?

Today take time to really observe the world around you. Take time to offer a prayer of thanks for the sky above and the beauty that lies beneath it. And take time to ponder the miracle of God's creation. The time you spend celebrating God's wonderful world is always time well spent.

> *Creation is filled with stunning variety and exquisite*
> *beauty. The delicate, intricate, and fragile,*
> *as well as the strong, mighty, and powerful,*
> *testify sweetly to the richness of the Creator.*
> Marilyn Meberg

What's Really Important

*Love not the world, neither the things that
are in the world. If any man love the world,
the love of the Father is not in him.*
1 John 2:15 KJV

Financial prosperity is a good thing, but spiritual prosperity is profoundly more important. Yet society often leads us to believe otherwise. The world seems to glorify material possessions, personal fame, and physical beauty above all else. But these things don't rank so highly with God. God sees the human heart—that's what's important to Him. And that's what should be important to you too.

As you establish your priorities for the coming day, remember this: the world will do everything it can to convince you that certain things are important. You'll be tempted to value fortune above faith, possessions above peace, and power above people. But if you'll listen, God will whisper in your heart the truth that faith, peace, and people are more important than fortune, possessions, and power. Listen to Him.

*People make a mistake in believing they're going
to be in paradise if they have more money.*
Mahalia Jackson

Clear Communication

*May the words of my mouth and the thoughts
of my heart be pleasing to you, O L ord,
my rock and my redeemer.*
Psalm 19:14 NLT

None other than Frank Sinatra once called Billie Holiday "the greatest influence on American popular singing" of his generation. Though her career was short, plagued by health problems and addiction, Ms. Holiday forever changed the world of American jazz.

Billie summed up her performances this way: "When I sing a tune and feel it, you can bet the audience will feel it too." That's true with more than just singing. The next time you want to get your message across, remember that excitement is contagious—and so is apathy.

Whether you're a teacher, salesperson, manager, or parent, your audience won't get excited about your message until you do.

There are many ways to communicate without actually speaking. Nonverbal communication and body language can convey as much, if not more, than speech.
Charmaine Saunders

Encouraging Words from the Wise

There is healing in the words of the wise.
Proverbs 12:18 MSG

Here's a question only you can answer: during a typical day, how many opportunities will you have to encourage other human beings? Unless you're living on a deserted island, the answer is "a lot!" And here's a follow-up question: how often do you take advantage of those opportunities? Hopefully, the answer is "more often than not."

Romans 14:19 advises us to "pursue what promotes peace and what builds up one another" (HCSB). And whenever we do, God smiles.

Whether you realize it or not, you're surrounded by people who need an encouraging word, a helping hand, or a pat on the back. And every time you encourage one of these folks, you'll be doing God's will by obeying God's Word. So with no further ado, let the encouragement begin.

Once you loosen up, let yourself be who you are: the wonderful, witty woman whom God will use to encourage and uplift other people.
Barbara Johnson

Wise Choices

*Daniel purposed in his heart that
he would not defile himself.*
Daniel 1:8 KJV

Each day we make countless choices that can bring us into a closer communion with God . . . or not. When we choose wisely, we earn blessings for ourselves and our loved ones. But when we make unwise choices—or hurtful ones—we invite old man trouble to drop by the house and stay awhile.

When we have a particularly tough decision to make, the best way to go about it is to seek God's wisdom and to trust it. We must pay careful attention to the conscience God has placed in our hearts. When we do, we will make wise decisions that improve our lives and the lives of those we love.

*In the long run, we shape our lives,
and we shape ourselves. And the choices
we make are ultimately our own responsibility.*
Eleanor Roosevelt

Serving Others with Love

*I tell you the truth, anything you did for even
the least of my people here, you also did for me.*
Matthew 25:40 NCV

The most esteemed men and women are not the
leaders of society or the captains of industry—
the greatest among us are those who choose to
minister and to serve.

Today you may feel the temptation to build
yourself up in the eyes of your neighbors. Resist that
temptation. Instead, serve others quietly and without
fanfare. Find a need and humbly fill it. Anonymously
lend a helping hand. Share a word of kindness.

When you take time to minister to those in need,
when you've done your best to serve your neighbors
and to serve your God, you can rest comfortably
knowing that in His eyes you have achieved
greatness.

*If you want to influence others to serve and help you
make a difference, you will get back what you give out.
The service ethic always boomerangs.*
Sheila Murray Bethel

Plans: Yours and God's

The LORD will do what is good in his sight.
1 Chronicles 19:13 NIV

All of us must, from time to time, endure days filled with suffering and pain. And as human beings with limited understanding, we seldom fully understand the plans of our Father in heaven. But we must learn to trust Him.

Corrie ten Boom understood that her own ability to understand the ebbs and flows of life was limited—but that God's is not. She said, "O Lord, thank You that Your side of the embroidery of our life is always perfect. That is such a comfort when our side is sometimes so mixed up."

When facing trials and tribulations, it's easy to ask, "Why me?" But even on life's dark days, you can be comforted by the knowledge that God is in charge and that He has plans for you . . . very good plans.

> *I'm convinced that there is nothing that can happen to me in this life that is not precisely designed by a sovereign Lord to give me the opportunity to learn to know Him.*
> Elisabeth Elliot

Above and Beyond Worry

> *I was very worried, but you comforted me.*
> Psalm 94:19 NCV

If you're like most women, it is simply a fact of life: from time to time you worry. You worry about health, about finances, about safety, about relationships, about family, and about countless other challenges in life, some great and some small. Where is the best place to take your worries? Take them to God. Take your troubles and your fears and your sorrows to Him.

Author Barbara Johnson said, "Worry is the senseless process of cluttering up tomorrow's opportunities with leftover problems from today."

If you'd like to make the most out of this day (and every one hereafter), turn your worries over to a power greater than yourself and spend your valuable time and energy solving the problems you can fix—while trusting God to do the rest.

> *Worry is stewing without doing!*
> Author Unknown

Big Dreams, Big God

You are the God who works wonders;
You revealed Your strength among the peoples.
Psalm 77:14 HCSB

How big are your dreams? Are you willing to contemplate the possibility that God has REALLY big things in store for you? Hopefully so, because the quality of your future may by closely correlated to the quality and the size of your dreams.

If you wake up each morning with a smile on your face, with hope in your heart, and with big dreams stretching your intellect, you're more likely to make those dreams come true. But if you spend more time (and energy) dreading the future than you spend preparing for the future, you'll be tempted to give up on your dreams without a fight.

So summon the courage to dream, and then get busy doing whatever work is required to make your dream come true. When you do, you'll discover that no dream is too big for God . . . *or* for you.

When we can't dream any longer, we die.
Emma Goldman

Creativity and Reinvention

You are being renewed in the spirit of your minds.
Ephesians 4:23 HCSB

Margaret Fuller learned Latin and Greek at age six and read Shakespeare by age eight. She made history in 1845 with the first known feminist writings in America. She was also a student of Ralph Waldo Emerson, a renowned author, editor, and literary critic.

Margaret once said, "An original mind is rarely understood." She knew from personal experience that creativity is sometimes a lonely burden, but that it also has its rewards.

The next time you encounter resistance to your original idea, whether at work or at home, stand up for your beliefs. And if you think that there are no more creative ideas to explore in your own life, take off the blinders and start reinventing yourself. Then prepare for a fresh round of success.

When the spirit of child's play enters into the creative process, it's a wonderful force and something to be nurtured.
Joni Mitchell

The Value of Friendship

Love one another earnestly from a pure heart.
1 Peter 1:22 HCSB

Emily Dickinson spoke for friends everywhere when she wrote, "My friends are my estate." She understood that friends are among our most treasured possessions. But unlike a bank account or a stock certificate, the value of a true friendship is beyond measure.

Today celebrate the joys of building and preserving your personal estate of lifelong friends. Give thanks for the laughter, the loyalty, the sharing, and the trust. Remember what it means to aid an ally, to be a backer, or to console a comrade. Pick up the telephone and reconnect with a long-lost pal. When you do, you will have increased two personal fortunes at once. And that's smart estate planning.

We have really no absent friends.
Elizabeth Bowen

Here for a Reason

> LORD, *You are our Father;*
> *we are the clay, and You are our potter;*
> *we all are the work of Your hands.*
> Isaiah 64:8 HCSB

Every person on earth (including you) is here for a reason. And the sooner you discover what it is you're here to do, the better. But sometimes your vision may be clouded by the inevitable complications and distractions of life here in the twenty-first century.

Helen Keller once observed, "I believe that all through these dark and silent years, God has been using my life for a purpose I do not know. But one day I will understand, and then I will be satisfied."

You, like Helen Keller, are here for a reason. God created you for a purpose, and He'll do His part to help you find it. In turn, God asks you to make your life a mission, not an intermission. So get busy. Your time on earth is limited, but your possibilities are not.

> *I would rather die a meaningful death*
> *than to live a meaningless life.*
> Corazón Aquino

Unafraid to Fail

> *Be strong and brave.*
> *Don't ever be afraid or discouraged!*
> Joshua 1:9 CEV

We live in a society that places a high value on success—a society that praises its victors and denigrates its vanquished. Perhaps that's why many of us are so afraid of failing. Yet here's a paradox: it is only when we become willing to "fail" that we become fully prepared to succeed.

For women struggling to be successful, cosmetics mogul Mary Kay Ash had this advice: "Fail forwards toward success." These words remind us that, although failure is an inevitable part of life, it need never be permanent.

So if you've experienced a setback or two, or even three, don't get down; get busy—busy searching for your next great adventure. Because failure is never final . . . unless you give up on yourself.

> *Many things are lost for want of asking.*
> English Proverb

Courage in a Fearful World

Let not your heart be troubled, neither let it be afraid.
John 14:27 KJV

We live in a world where bad news travels at lightning speed (and good news doesn't). These are troubled times, times when we have legitimate fears for the future of our nation, our world, and our families. Yet we have every reason to live courageously.

Perhaps you've found your courage tested by the anxieties that are an inevitable part of twenty-first-century life. If so, God wants to have a little chat with you. He wants to remind you that even when you find your courage waning, He is with you.

Your heavenly Father is your protector and your deliverer. Call on Him today and be comforted. Whatever the size of your fear, God is bigger.

Fear knocked at the door. Faith answered.
No one was there.
Author Unknown

Your Conscience, God's Voice

Behold, the kingdom of God is within you.
Luke 17:21 KJV

Evangelist Billy Graham observed, "Most of us follow our conscience as we follow a wheelbarrow. We push it in front of us in the direction we want to go." To do so, of course, is a profound mistake. Yet all of us, on occasion, have failed to listen to the voice God embedded in our hearts—and all of us have suffered the consequences.

God gave you a conscience for good reason: to make your life better, safer, and easier. And if you're wise, you'll listen carefully to that inner voice.

When your conscience speaks, listen and learn. In all likelihood, God is trying to get His message through. And it's surely a message you desperately need to hear.

> *One's conscience can only be satisfied when God is satisfied.*
> Charles H. Spurgeon

Making Time for God

First pay attention to me, and then relax.
Now you can take it easy—you're in good hands.
Proverbs 1:33 MSG

Daily life is a tapestry of habits, and no habit is more important to your spiritual health than the discipline of daily prayer and devotion to God. When you begin each day with your head bowed and your heart lifted, you'll be reminded of the Creator's love and of His laws. If you find that you're simply too busy for a daily chat with your heavenly Father, it's an indicator that you probably need to take a long, hard look at your values and how you're spending your time.

If you've acquired the unfortunate habit of trying to squeeze God into the corners of your life, reshuffle the items on your to-do list and put God first. He wants your undivided attention, not the leftovers of your day. Form (or renew) the habit of spending quality time with your Creator. He'll make it worth your while.

God calls us to seek Him daily
in order to serve Him daily.
Sheila Cragg

August 28

When People Behave Badly

A fool's wrath is known at once,
but a prudent man covers shame.
Proverbs 12:16 NKJV

Sometimes people can be discourteous and cruel. Sometimes they can be unfair, unkind, and unappreciative. Sometimes people get angry and frustrated. So what are we to do? God's answer is straightforward: forgive, forget, and move on. Luke 6:37 says, "Do not judge, and you will not be judged. Do not condemn, and you will not be condemned. Forgive, and you will be forgiven" (HCSB).

Today and every day be quick to forgive others for their shortcomings. And when people misbehave (as they most certainly will from time to time), don't pay too much attention. Just forgive those people as quickly as you can, and try to move on . . . and when you misbehave, maybe they'll do the same for you.

We are all fallen creatures and
all very hard to live with.
C. S. Lewis

The Need for Discipline

It is better to have self-control than to conquer a city.
Proverbs 16:32 NLT

Wise women understand the importance of discipline. In Proverbs 28:19 the principle is clear: "Those who work their land will have plenty of food, but the ones who chase empty dreams instead will end up poor" (NCV).

If we work diligently and faithfully, we can expect a bountiful harvest. But we must never expect the harvest to precede the labor.

Poet Mary Frances Butts advised, "Build a little fence of trust around today. Fill each space with loving work, and therein stay."

Thoughtful women understand that God doesn't accept laziness. He expects His children (of all ages) to lead disciplined lives. But when they do, He rewards them.

Real freedom means to welcome the responsibility
it brings, to welcome the God-control it requires,
to welcome the discipline that results,
to welcome the maturity it creates.
Eugenia Price

Inspiring Others

*Let us consider how to stimulate one another
to love and good deeds.*
Hebrews 10:24 NASB

As a woman you are a continuing source of encouragement to your family and friends. After all, one of the reasons God put you here is to serve and encourage other people—starting with the people who live under your roof.

How can you help build up other people's confidence? By celebrating their victories and their accomplishments. As the saying goes, "When someone does something good, applaud—you'll make two people happy."

Look for the good in others today, and celebrate the good you find. When you do, you'll be a powerful force of encouragement in your corner of the world—and the world needs all the encouragement it can get.

*What are God's servants but His minstrels,
who must inspire the hearts of men
and stir them to spiritual joy!*
Saint Francis of Assisi

Your Positive Influence

*Instruct and direct one another
using good common sense.*
Colossians 3:16 MSG

All of us serve as powerful examples to young people, friends, and family members. That's a lot of influence and a big responsibility.

Daniel Webster wrote, "If we work in marble, it will perish; if we work upon brass, time will efface it; but if we work upon immortal minds and instill in them just principles, we are then engraving upon tablets which no time will efface, but which will brighten and brighten to all eternity."

What a great reminder of the glorious opportunities available to all of us whenever we're willing to serve as positive role models.

God has placed people along your path, people He intends for you to influence. Every time you serve as a good example, you help to reshape the world into a better place.

*There is a transcendent power in example.
We reform others unconsciously
when we walk uprightly.*
Anne Sophie Swetchine

September

Caring for Your Family

*These should learn first of all to put their religion
into practice by caring for their own family.*
1 Timothy 5:4 NIV

A s you consider God's purpose for your life, you
must also consider how your plans will affect
the most important people God has entrusted to
your care: your loved ones.

Our families and friends are precious gifts from
our Father in heaven. We must care for and make
time for them, even when the demands of the day are
great. In a world filled with countless obligations and
frequent frustrations, we may be tempted to take our
families and friends for granted. But God wants us to
honor Him by honoring our loved ones—by giving
them our support, our time, and our cooperation.

No relationships, and no people, are perfect. But
imperfect as they may be, your family and friends are
God's blessings to you, and they need and deserve
your care.

*[God] intended families to be the safe haven
where children are born and raised,
a place where the tender shoots are nurtured
until their roots grow strong and deep.*
Carol Kuykendall

Sharing Your Talents

There are varieties of gifts,
but the same Spirit. And there are varieties
of ministries, and the same Lord.
1 Corinthians 12:4–5 NASB

God has given you an array of talents, and He has given you unique opportunities to share those talents with the world. Now it's your job to use those talents and to use them well.

The saying is both familiar and true: "What you are is God's gift to you; what you become is your gift to God." The implication is clear: you must strive to make the most of your own God-given talents.

Today make this promise to yourself: vow to share your talents as a gift to your family, to your friends, and to the world. And remember: the best way to say thank you for God's gifts is to use them.

Whether we are poets or parents or teachers or artists
or gardeners, we must start where we are and use what
we have. In the process of creation and relationship,
what seems mundane and trivial may show itself
to be holy, precious, part of a pattern.
Luci Shaw

Getting to the Other Side of Anger

*Those who control their anger have great
understanding; those with
a hasty temper will make mistakes.*
Proverbs 14:29 NLT

Anger is a natural human emotion that is sometimes necessary and appropriate. Righteous indignation, for example, is an appropriate response to evil. But God does not intend that anger should rule our lives. Far from it. God tells us to turn away from anger and to forgive our neighbors.

Today decide to turn away from anger, hatred, bitterness, frustration, and regret. Be quick to forgive imperfections—other people's and your own.

Turning from anger does not mean "repressing" it; rather, it means acknowledging its existence, and perhaps even its validity, but then choosing to put that anger aside. As you open your heart to forgiveness and get to the other side of anger, you'll find peace.

*Anger repressed can poison a relationship as
surely as the cruelest words.*
Dr. Joyce Brothers

Believe in Yourself

It is pleasant to see dreams come true.
Proverbs 13:19 NLT

It took this Atlanta native ten long years to complete her fictional account of the Civil War. And then she was reluctant to have the book published because she feared it wasn't good enough. The novel that took Margaret Mitchell so long to complete was *Gone with the Wind*, one of the best-selling books and most popular movies of all time.

If you're working toward a big goal but are afraid that your efforts may not measure up, remember Margaret Mitchell. Don't pay too much attention to occasional bouts of self-doubt. Your work is probably better than you think. And unless you give up on yourself, your dreams are never gone with the wind.

Now is the operative word. Everything you put in your way is just a method of putting off the hour when you could actually be doing your dream. You don't need endless time and perfect conditions.
Barbara Sher

The Wisdom to Be Humble

*Don't be afraid. From the moment you decided
to humble yourself to receive
understanding, your prayer was heard.*
Daniel 10:12 MSG

Humility is not, in most cases, a natural human trait. Most of us are more than willing to take a generous view of our own accomplishments. We're tempted to say, "Look how wonderful I am!" hoping the world will agree with our self-appraisals.

But God honors humility, and He rewards those who humbly serve Him. When we acquire the wisdom to be humble, we bring enlightenment to the world and blessings to ourselves. If we can't overcome the tendency to overestimate our own achievements, God still has some important lessons to teach us— lessons about the wisdom, the power, and the beauty of humility.

*The gate of heaven is very low;
only the humble can enter it.*
Saint Elizabeth Ann Seton

Hugs Now!

*If I have the gift of prophecy, and understand
all mysteries and all knowledge,
and if I have all faith, so that I can move mountains,
but do not have love, I am nothing.*
1 Corinthians 13:2 HCSB

When is the best time to share a hug with a friend or family member? Almost anytime is a good time, but when it comes to hugs, sooner is better than later.

When you demonstrate your love with words, hugs, or smiles, you are helping to make God's world a kinder, gentler place. And that's exactly what God wants you to do.

C. S. Lewis said, "Love, either towards God or towards man, is an affair of the will." Are you willing to slow down and demonstrate your affection to the people God has placed along your path? Hopefully so, because all those people need hugs—now! And you'll enjoy the ones you get in return.

A hug is the ideal gift . . . one size fits all.
Author Unknown

Sufficient for Your Needs

This same God who takes care of me
will supply all your needs from his glorious riches.
Philippians 4:19 NLT

Of this you can be sure: God is sufficient to meet your needs. Whatever dangers you may face, whatever setbacks you must endure, God is with you, and He stands ready to protect you.

The psalmist wrote, "Weeping may endure for a night, but joy comes in the morning" (Psalm 30:5 NKJV). When we're suffering, though, the morning may seem far away. Yet God promises that He is "near to those who have a broken heart" (Psalm 34:18 NKJV).

If you're experiencing the intense pain of a recent loss, or if you're still mourning a loss from long ago, perhaps the time has come to trust God and to reclaim the wonderful life He has in store for you.

His strength is made perfect,
not in our strength, but in our weakness.
Hannah Whitall Smith

When It's Difficult to Be Kind

See that no one renders evil for evil to anyone,
but always pursue what is good
both for yourselves and for all.
1 Thessalonians 5:15 NKJV

Sometimes it's difficult to be kind. But amid the stressful moments of your demanding days, you've slowed down long enough to sow seeds of kindness. And you can be sure your friends and family members have been blessed by your compassion.

The philosopher Seneca wrote, "Wherever there is a human being, there is an opportunity for kindness." You have used countless opportunities to share a kind word or to lend a helping hand. Thank you!

Swiss critic Henri Frédéric Amiel gave this wise counsel: "Life is short, and we have not too much time for gardening the hearts of those who are traveling the dark way with us. Oh, be swift to love! Make haste to be kind." As a compassionate woman, you have always been a little kinder than necessary. And your generosity has not gone unnoticed.

The future belongs to those who live
and love in the present moment.
Author Unknown

Forget It

*Should we accept only good from God
and not adversity?*
Job 2:10 HCSB

Nancy Lopez is a member of the LPGA Hall of Fame and one of the most popular golfers in history. After earning more than her share of wins, Nancy had this advice about losing: "The first thing I do after losing a match is forget it." That's a timely tip for life on the golf course and life beyond the eighteenth green.

The next time you fall a little short, whether at work, home, or school, learn from your mistakes, but don't focus on them. You can't win this round if you're preoccupied with the previous one. No one wins them all, not even Nancy Lopez. But if you keep your mind in the right place, you'll be sure to win your share.

You may encounter many defeats, but you must not be defeated. In fact, it may be necessary to encounter the defeats, so you can know who you are and what you can rise above.
Maya Angelou

Habits for Life

Wisdom is a tree of life to those who embrace her;
happy are those who hold her tightly.
Proverbs 3:18 NLT

If you sincerely desire to improve your health and to make those improvements stick, take an honest look at the habits that make up the fabric of your day.

American philosopher Eric Hoffer observed, "Wise living consists perhaps less in acquiring good habits than in acquiring as few bad habits as possible."

Are you eating unhealthy foods without even thinking about the consequences? It's time to change. Are you addicted to cigarettes? It's time to quit. Do you constantly dwell on negative thoughts? It's time to think more critically about what you're focusing on.

Your habits help determine the quality and tone of your day. If you make those habits work for you, you'll be surprised at how quickly your health will begin to improve.

It is easier to stay out than to get out.
Author Unknown

Being Patient with Yourself

Be patient with everyone.
1 Thessalonians 5:14 NASB

Being patient with other people can be difficult. But sometimes we find it even more difficult to be patient with ourselves. We have high expectations and lofty goals. We want to accomplish things now, not later. We want our lives to unfold according to our own timetables. But what about God's timetable? His timetable for our lives is much better than our own.

Patience and wisdom go hand in hand. And for most of us, learning the art of patience means learning how to be patient, not only with other people, but also with ourselves.

Your task, then, is clear: be patient with all people, beginning—not surprisingly—with the woman who stares back at you each time you gaze into the mirror.

We are so used to living in an instant world that it is difficult to wait for anything.
Kay Arthur

Mastering Money

The love of money is the root of all evil.
1 Timothy 6:10 KJV

Our society holds material possessions in high regard. Far too many people seem to worship money and the things money can buy, yet such misplaced priorities usually lead to disappointment and dissatisfaction. Popular opinion to the contrary, money cannot buy happiness.

Money, in and of itself, is not evil; but the love of money inevitably leads to troublesome behavior. So today, as you prioritize matters of importance for you and yours, remember that God is almighty—the dollar is not.

Circus master P. T. Barnum observed, "Money is a terrible master but a wonderful servant." You must master money or be mastered by it. The choice is yours.

Have you prayed about your resources lately?
Find out how God wants you
to use your time and your money.
Kay Arthur

September 13

Your Glorious Opportunities

*Whenever we have the opportunity,
we should do good to everyone.*
Galatians 6:10 NLT

Are you excited about the opportunities of today and thrilled by the possibilities of tomorrow? Do you confidently expect God to lead you to a place of abundance, peace, and joy? You should be. After all, you're surrounded by countless opportunities to improve your own life and the lives of those you love.

Today, as you prepare to meet the duties of everyday life, pause and consider what glorious opportunities await. Then think for a moment about your potential to make the world a better place.

You can do many things to make your life—and your world—happier, kinder, and gentler. And that's precisely what God wants you to do, starting now.

*I do not weep at the world—
I am too busy sharpening my oyster knife.*
Zora Neale Hurston

A Happy Ending

They won't be afraid of bad news;
their hearts are steady because they trust the LORD.
Psalm 112:7 NCV

At the peak of her career, Mary Pickford was called "America's sweetheart." In 1919, along with Charlie Chaplin, Douglas Fairbanks, and D. W. Griffith, she formed United Artists Corporation, a Hollywood powerhouse. Mary made this simple yet powerful statement: "Failure isn't falling down, it's staying down." She understood that nothing succeeds at bringing about a happy ending like persistence.

From time to time life knocks everybody down, and you'll be no exception. But it's up to you to decide whether you'll stay down or get back up again. If you're persistent, you can outwait and outwork failure. Then, like those Mary Pickford movies, you'll find a very happy ending.

Start by doing what's necessary, then what's possible,
and suddenly you are doing the impossible.
Saint Francis of Assisi

The Inner Voice

*God is pleased with you when, for the sake of
your conscience, you patiently endure unfair treatment.*
1 Peter 2:19 NLT

The legendary actress Loretta Young once said, "If you listen to your conscience, it will serve you as no other friend you'll ever know." How true. Even when we deceive our neighbors, and even when we try to deceive ourselves, God has given each of us a conscience—a small, quiet voice that tells us right from wrong. We must listen to that inner voice, or accept the consequences.

Have you acquired the habit of listening carefully to that still, small voice God has placed in your heart? If not, it's time to start, because God put it there for a very good reason: to use it. And the best moment to use it is always the present one.

*While conscience is our friend, all is at peace; however
once it is offended, farewell to a tranquil mind.*
Lady Mary Wortley Montagu

Being Gentle with Yourself

A devout life does bring wealth,
but it's the rich simplicity of
being yourself before God.
1 Timothy 6:6 MSG

A re you your own worst critic? Why not try being a little more understanding of the woman you see whenever you look into the mirror?

Millions of words have been written about various ways to improve self-image and increase self-esteem. Yet maintaining a healthy self-image is largely a matter of doing three things: behaving ourselves, thinking healthy thoughts, and finding a purpose in life that pleases your Creator and yourself.

God accepts us just as we are, and self-acceptance is a part of His will for all of us. If God accepts us—faults and all—then who are we to do otherwise?

Change occurs when one becomes what she is,
not when she tries to become what she is not.
Ruth P. Freedman

Embracing Serenity

The work of righteousness will be peace, and the service of righteousness, quietness and confidence forever.
Isaiah 32:17 NASB

Are you embittered by circumstances you didn't deserve and can't understand? Sometimes the best cure is to accept the unchangeable past and to have faith in the promise of tomorrow. Now is the time to trust God completely and to reclaim the peace—His peace—that can and should be yours.

God understands your situation even when you don't. And He has a reason for everything He does. But God doesn't usually explain His workings in ways that we, as mortals with limited insight and clouded vision, can comprehend. So instead of understanding every aspect of the Father's unfolding plan for our lives and our universe, we must be satisfied to trust Him. We may not be able to know the details, but we can embrace serenity by leaving those details in His capable hands.

God, give us the serenity to accept what cannot be changed. Give us courage to change what should be changed. Give us the wisdom to distinguish one from the other.
Reinhold Niebuhr

The Power of a Plan

Teach me to do thy will; for thou art my God:
thy Spirit is good; lead me into the land of uprightness.
Psalm 143:10 KJV

If you have no idea where you want to go, any road will take you there. And if you're determined to live a life of total spontaneity, a life devoid of planning and preparation, good luck. But if you're like most people, you'll achieve greater contentment and success by planning for the future. In fact, a clearly marked road map for life can be a powerful tool for achieving the things you want and need.

Life is uncertain, of course, but uncertainty is no excuse for fuzzy thinking or sloppy planning. That's why you should invest ample time planning for this day and each day that follows. Then you can summon the energy and the courage required to implement your plans, come what may.

Goals are a joint effort process: getting in touch
with our heart and setting a course;
then depending on and being willing
for God to direct us one step at a time.
Sheila West

Happy Trails

Fear not, for I have redeemed you;
I have called you by your name; you are Mine.
Isaiah 43:1 NKJV

Considered by some to be the most popular cowgirl of her time, Dale Evans starred with cowboy husband Roy Rogers, and she wrote their theme song, "Happy Trails." This trailblazer said, "I have found the perfect antidote for fear. Whenever it sticks up its ugly face, I clobber it with prayer."

Psalm 118:5 says, "In my distress I prayed to the Lord, and the Lord answered me and rescued me" (NLT). And He'll do the same for you. If you've been beset by the inevitable disappointments and fears that grip us all from time to time, pray for courage—and keep praying. When you do, you'll find plenty of clear skies and lots of happy trails.

I am not afraid of storms,
for I am learning how to sail my ship.
Louisa May Alcott

Whistle While You Work

> *So I recommend having fun . . . .*
> *That way they will experience some happiness*
> *along with all the hard work God gives them.*
> Ecclesiastes 8:15 NLT

Are you a woman who takes time each day to really enjoy life? Hopefully so. After all, you are the recipient of a precious gift—the gift of life. And because God has seen fit to give you this gift, it is incumbent upon you to use it and to enjoy it. But sometimes, amid the pressures of everyday living, really enjoying life may seem almost impossible. It is not.

For most of us, fun is as much a function of attitude as it is a function of environment. So make it a choice daily to enjoy yourself. Today is God's gift to you, and He wants you to find joy in it . . . so what on earth are you waiting for?

The present is a present. Unwrap it.
Marie T. Freeman

A Hug and a Helping Hand

*If you give, you will receive. Your gift will return to
you in full measure, pressed down, shaken together
to make room for more, and running over.
Whatever measure you use in giving—large or small—
it will be used to measure what is given back to you.*
Luke 6:38 NLT

Most of us have heard the story of the good
Samaritan, a man who helped a fellow
traveler when no one else would. We too should
be good Samaritans when we encounter others
who need help.

Zora Neale Hurston once said, "When you find
a man who has lost his way, you don't make fun of
him and scorn him and leave him there. You show
him the way. If you don't do that, you just prove that
you're sort of lost yourself."

Her insight fits well with the antidote in Helen
Keller's advice: "Believe, when you are most unhappy, that there is something for you to do in the
world. So long as you can sweeten another's pain,
life is not in vain."

Find someone today who needs a hug or a helping
hand and give them both.

*If a lion's roar isn't getting you anyplace,
try a bear hug.*
Author Unknown

Choices That Please God

I am offering you life or death, blessings or curses. Now, choose life! . . . To choose life is to love the LORD your God, obey him, and stay close to him.
Deuteronomy 30:19–20 NCV

Life presents each of us with questions, conundrums, doubts, and problems. Thankfully, the riddles of everyday living are not too difficult to solve if we look for answers in the right places. When we have choices to make, we can look to the counsel of God-fearing friends and family members.

Are you facing a difficult decision? Take your concerns to God and avail yourself of the messages and mentors He has placed along your path. When you do, God will speak to you in His own way and in His own time. And you can trust the answers He gives.

We need to teach the next generation of children from Day One that they are responsible for their lives. Mankind's greatest gift, also its greatest curse, is that we have free choice. We can make our choices built from love or from fear.
Elisabeth Kübler-Ross

A Growing Relationship with God

This is why I remind you to keep using the gift
God gave you. . . . Now let it grow,
as a small flame grows into a fire.
2 Timothy 1:6 NCV

Your relationship with God is ongoing; it unfolds day by day, and it offers countless opportunities to grow closer to Him . . . or to move away from Him. Each day you're confronted with a wide range of decisions: how you will behave, where you will direct your thoughts, with whom you will associate, and what you will choose to worship. These choices, along with many others like them, are yours and yours alone. How you choose determines how your relationship with God will develop.

Are you continuing to grow in your relationship with God? Hopefully, you're determined to make yourself spiritually mature. The rewards are worth the effort.

Spiritual freedom is the state of having become
childlike with God. Not childish, childlike.
Eugenia Price

September 24

The New You

*We are asking that you may be filled with
the knowledge of His will in all wisdom
and spiritual understanding.*
Colossians 1:9 HCSB

God has the power to transform your life if you invite Him to do so. It's your decision, and it's straightforward: whether to allow the Father's transforming power to work in you and through you.

Sometimes the demands of daily life may drain you of strength or rob you of the joy that is rightfully yours. But even on your busiest day—or your darkest—you can be comforted by the knowledge that God has the power to renew your spirit and your life.

Are you in need of a new beginning? Turn your heart toward God. When you do, you'll discover that the Creator of the universe is in the business of making all things new—including you.

If you surrender to the wind, you can ride it.
Toni Morrison

Talking Respectfully . . . to Yourself

*A devout life does bring wealth, but it's the rich
simplicity of being yourself before God.*
1 Timothy 6:6 MSG

What are you telling yourself about yourself? When you look in the mirror, are you staring back at your biggest booster or your harshest critic? If you can learn to give yourself the benefit of the doubt—if you can speak respectfully and constructively to the woman in the mirror—then you'll benefit from those conversations. But if you're constantly berating yourself—if you're constantly telling yourself that you simply don't measure up—then you'll find that your sense of self-worth will suffer.

If you've acquired the habit of thinking constructively about yourself and your circumstances, congratulations. But if you're mired in the mental quicksand of overly self-critical thoughts, it's time to change your thoughts and, by doing so, your life.

Such as I am, I am a precious gift.
Zora Neale Hurston

The Storms of Life

*God doesn't want us to be shy with his gifts,
but bold and loving and sensible.*
2 Timothy 1:7 MSG

A storm rose quickly on the Sea of Galilee, and Jesus's disciples were afraid. Although they had seen Him perform many miracles, the disciples feared for their lives. They turned to Him, and He calmed the waters and the wind.

Sometimes we, like the disciples, feel threatened by the inevitable storms of life. And when we're fearful, we, too, can turn to our Lord for courage and for comfort.

The next time you're afraid, remember the One who calmed the wind and the waves. And remember that He can calm all the storms of life, including yours.

*God did away with all my fear.
It was time for someone to stand up—
or in my case, sit down. So I refused to move.*
Rosa Parks

Expecting the Best

> *Let's keep a firm grip on the promises that*
> *keep us going. He always keeps his word.*
> Hebrews 10:23 MSG

As each day unfolds, we are literally surrounded by more opportunities than we can count—opportunities to improve our own lives and the lives of those we love. Each of us possesses the ability to experience earthly peace and spiritual abundance, but sometimes peace and abundance seem to be little more than distant promises.

Do you expect the coming day to be a fountain of opportunities? Are you expecting the best and preparing yourself for it, or are you expecting the worst and bracing yourself against it?

As we face the challenges that are part of life here on earth, we must not become discouraged. We must, instead, arm ourselves with the promises of God. When we do, we can expect the very best that life—and God—has to offer.

> *The meaning of hope isn't just some flimsy wishing.*
> *It's a firm confidence in God's promises—*
> *that He will ultimately set things right.*
> Sheila Walsh

Thinking Clearly

*Think clearly and exercise self-control.
Look forward to the special blessings
that will come to you.*
1 Peter 1:13 NLT

Our thoughts are powerful things. They can lift us up or drag us down. They have the power to energize us or deplete us, to inspire us to greater accomplishments or render our goals unreachable.

Bishop Fulton Sheen said, "The mind is like a clock that is constantly running down. It needs to be wound up daily with good thoughts." But sometimes, even for the most faithful believers, winding up our intellectual clocks is difficult.

If negative thoughts have left you worried, exhausted, or both, it's time to readjust your thought patterns. Negative thinking is habit-forming; but thankfully, so is positive thinking. It's up to you to train your mind to focus on God's power and your possibilities. Both are far greater than you can imagine.

*Be very careful what thoughts you put
into your mind. For good or bad,
they will boomerang right back to you.*
Beatryce Nivens

Ousting Envy

*Where envy and self-seeking exist,
confusion and every evil thing are there.*
James 3:16 NKJV

Because we're imperfect, we're sometimes envious of others. But to be envious is to be foolish. We must guard against the natural tendency to feel resentment and jealousy when other people experience good fortune.

Rather than succumbing to feelings of envy, we should focus on the marvelous things God has done for us (and we should refrain from preoccupying ourselves with the blessings God has chosen to give others).

Saint John Chrysostom offered these words of caution: "As a moth gnaws a garment, so does envy consume a man." So here's a proven formula for a happier, healthier life: count your own blessings, and let your neighbors count theirs. It's the best way to live.

*Never indulge in jealousy or envy.
Those two destructive emotions will eat you alive.*
Loretta Young

Transcendent Love

The Lord is full of compassion and mercy.
James 5:11 NIV

Where can we find God's love? Everywhere. His love transcends space and time. It reaches beyond the heavens, and it touches the darkest, smallest corner of every human heart. When we sincerely open our minds and hearts to God, His love does not arrive someday—it arrives immediately.

Speaker Joyce Meyer reminds us, "God has the marvelous ability to love us in the midst of our imperfections." And if He can love us unconditionally, we should find the wisdom and the courage to love ourselves, come what may.

Take God at His word and welcome His love into your heart today. When you do, His transcendent love will surround you now and always.

I am grateful that when even a single sparrow falls to the ground, God knows—and understands.
Ruth Bell Graham

October

Beyond the Status Quo

Staying with it—that's what God requires.
Stay with it to the end. You won't be sorry.
Matthew 24:13 MSG

She didn't just sing her way out of poverty, she worked her way out. But it took courage for this young woman to follow her dreams. In the early days she and her husband, Mooney, traveled the rural South promoting her records. But they were so poor that they slept in the backseat of their car and lived on a steady diet of bologna sandwiches.

Eventually, the hard work paid off, and Loretta Lynn forged a hall-of-fame career. When questioned about her success, Loretta had this advice: "You've got to keep growing, or you're just like last night's corn bread: stale and dry."

If you'd like to give your life a boost, keep working, keep dreaming, and avoid the status quo. After all, if there's anything worse than stale corn bread, it's stale people.

Attitude is contagious. Is yours worth catching?
Author Unknown

Listening to God's Voice

*God has no use for the prayers
of the people who won't listen to him.*
Proverbs 28:9 MSG

Sometimes God speaks loudly and clearly. More often He speaks in a quiet voice, and if you're wise, you'll be listening carefully when He does. But to do so, you must set aside quiet moments each day to sense His direction.

Can you quiet yourself long enough to listen to His voice? Are you attuned to the subtle guidance of your intuition? Are you willing to pray sincerely and then to wait quietly for God's response? Hopefully so, because He doesn't usually send messages on stone tablets or city billboards. He communicates in subtler ways. If you sincerely desire to hear His voice, you must listen carefully, in the silent corners of your quiet, willing heart.

*Wait before the Lord. Wait in the stillness.
And in that stillness, assurance will come to you.
You will know that you are heard; you will know that
your Lord ponders the voice of your humble desires.*
Amy Carmichael

Forgiving and Forgetting

*Be kind to each other, tenderhearted,
forgiving one another.*
Ephesians 4:32 NLT

When people behave badly, it's hard to forgive them. Sometimes it's impossible to forget the people who hurt our feelings. But even if we can't forget, we can forgive. And that's exactly what God teaches us to do.

What if you've already tried to forgive someone and simply can't seem to do it? Then you must keep trying. God instructs us to treat other people exactly as we wish to be treated. And since you want to be forgiven for the mistakes you make, you must be willing to extend forgiveness to other people for the mistakes that they've made. So if you can't seem to forgive someone, keep asking God to help you until you do. You can be sure that if you keep asking for His help, He will give it.

*The more you practice the art of forgiving,
the better you'll be at the art of living.*
Marie T. Freeman

A Blessed Life

If you understand what I'm telling you,
act like it—and live a blessed life.
John 13:17 MSG

If you sincerely wish to feel blessed, make thanksgiving a habit, a regular part of your daily routine.

How has God blessed you? Today take time to make a partial list of His gifts to you: the talents, the opportunities, the possessions, and the relationships that you may, on occasion, take for granted. Then, when you've spent sufficient time listing your blessings, offer a prayer of gratitude to the giver of all good things. And to the best of your ability, use your gifts for the betterment of yourself, your family, your friends, and your world. Then you'll truly live a blessed life.

Thanksgiving or complaining—these words express
two contrastive attitudes of the souls of God's children
in regard to His dealings with them. The soul that gives
thanks can find comfort in everything; the soul that
complains can find comfort in nothing.
Hannah Whitall Smith

God's Awesome Creation

Everything God does will remain forever;
there is nothing to add to it and
there is nothing to take from it.
Ecclesiastes 3:14 NASB

When we consider God's glorious universe, we marvel at the miracle of nature. The smallest seedlings and grandest stars are all part of God's infinite creation. He has placed His handiwork on display for all to see, and if we are wise, we will make time each day to celebrate the world that surrounds us.

As you fulfill the demands of your life today, pause to consider the majesty of heaven and earth. God's handiwork is as miraculous as it is beautiful, as incomprehensible as it is breathtaking.

The heavens are a declaration of God's glory. May we never cease to praise the Father for a universe that stands as an awesome testimony to His presence and His power.

The best remedy for those who are afraid, lonely,
or unhappy is to go outside, somewhere where they can
be quite alone with the heavens, nature, and God.
Anne Frank

A Lesson about Success

*We must not get tired of doing good, for we will
reap at the proper time if we don't give up.*
Galatians 6:9 HCSB

Actress Helen Hayes once said, "My mother drew a distinction between achievement and success. She said that achievement is the knowledge that you have studied and worked hard and done the best that is in you. Success is being praised by others. Success is nice but not as important or satisfying. Always aim for achievement and forget about success."

Helen's mother was wise, indeed.

The secret of success often lies in the ability to place more importance on achievement than on recognition. If you want to be a success, forget about being successful and concentrate instead on becoming the best you that you can be. Then success has a way of taking care of itself.

*Starting out to make money is the greatest mistake
in life. Do what you feel you have a flair for doing, and
if you are good enough at it, the money will come.*
Greer Garson

It's Up to You

> *"LORD, help!" they cried in their trouble,*
> *and he saved them.*
> Psalm 107:28 NLT

God has much to offer us, and He wants us to have the best He has to give. But sometimes we're simply unwilling or unable to accept the blessings God wants us to receive. Why? Because we fail to trust Him completely and because we are, at times, surprisingly stubborn. We just won't ask for His help.

Are you asking God to move mountains in your life, or are you only expecting Him to help you stumble over a few anthills? Whatever the size of your challenges, God is big enough to handle them. Whatever the extent of your need, He can meet it. But it's up to you. Ask for His wisdom and His guidance today, with faith and with fervor, and then watch in amazement as those mountains begin to move.

When trials come your way—as inevitably they will— do not run away. Run to your God and Father.
Kay Arthur

Conquering the Everyday Frustrations

He that will love life, and see good days,
let him refrain his tongue from evil,
and his lips that they speak no guile.
1 Peter 3:10 KJV

Perhaps God gave each of us one mouth and two ears in order that we might listen twice as much as we speak. Unfortunately, many of us do the opposite, especially when we become frustrated.

Frustration is a natural human emotion when things aren't going as we'd hoped or planned, when we feel thwarted. Some days we may feel as though the world is falling in on us, but more often than not our frustrations are of the more mundane variety.

As long as we live, we will daily be tempted to lose our tempers and spout off over small, relatively insignificant events: an inconsiderate driver, a spilled cup of milk, an unfortunate comment, a forgotten promise. These sorts of frustrations may irritate us, but they should not conquer us. We should conquer them.

To handle yourself, use your head. To handle others,
use your heart. Anger is only one letter short of danger.
Eleanor Roosevelt

Healthy Choices

*Dear friend, I pray that you may prosper in every way
and be in good health, just as your soul prospers.*
3 John 1:2 HCSB

Good health is not only a common-sense exercise in personal discipline, it is also a spiritual journey.

God does not intend that we abuse our bodies by giving in to excessive appetites or to slothful behavior—or to overwork either. To the contrary, God has instructed us to protect our physical bodies the best we can. To do otherwise is unwise and unsafe.

God has a plan for every aspect of your life, and His plan includes provisions for your spiritual, physical, and emotional health. But He expects you to do your fair share of the work. In a world that's chock-full of tasty temptations, it's all too easy to make unhealthy choices. But as you make the right kinds of choices, you'll gain new strength and health in both body and soul.

Avoid temptation and it will avoid you.
Author Unknown

Self-Fulfilling Prophecy

Hope deferred maketh the heart sick.
Proverbs 13:12 KJV

The self-fulfilling prophecy is alive, well, and living at your house. If you trust God and have faith for the future, your optimistic beliefs will give you direction and motivation. But if you allow negative thoughts to flourish, they will tend, over time, to become reality.

When you acquire the habit of hopeful thinking, you will have acquired a powerful tool for improving your life. So if you find yourself succumbing to worry and discouragement, seek God's healing touch and the encouraging words of friends and family. And if you fall into the harmful habit of negative thinking, just think again. After all, God teaches us that with His help we can overcome every difficulty. And when God makes a promise, He keeps it.

Ask for what you want and be prepared to get it.
Maya Angelou

Aiming Grandly

I will lift up my eyes to the hills—from whence comes my help? My help comes from the LORD, who made heaven and earth.
Psalm 121:1–2 NKJV

Jacqueline Kennedy Onassis was buried in Arlington National Cemetery next to her first husband, John F. Kennedy. Mrs. Kennedy had become one of America's most notable first ladies at the relatively young age of thirty-one. Five years after her husband's death, Jacqueline married shipping magnate Aristotle Onassis. Following her second marriage, "Jackie O," who had already been an international celebrity, became one of the most closely watched public figures in the world.

Jacqueline once observed, "A grand aim for one's life is the only fortune worth having." God created us to yearn for something grander that ourselves, and there's no grander aim than *knowing* God. He promises that if we *seek* Him, He will be *found*: "'I will be found by you,' declares the LORD (Jeremiah 29:14 NIV). Aim high—aim all the way up to heaven!

Do not stop thinking of life as an adventure. You have no security unless you live bravely, excitingly, imaginatively.
Eleanor Roosevelt

Your Spiritual Journey

Let us leave the elementary teachings . . .
and go on to maturity.
Hebrews 6:1 NIV

Complete spiritual maturity is never achieved in a day, or in a year, or even in a lifetime. The journey toward spiritual maturity is an ongoing process that continues, day by day, throughout every stage of life. Every stage of life has its opportunities and its challenges, and if we're wise, we continue to seek God's guidance as each new chapter of life unfolds. Norman Vincent Peale advised: "Ask the God who made you to keep remaking you." That counsel is perfectly sound, but easy to ignore.

When we cease to grow, either emotionally or spiritually, we do ourselves a profound disservice. But if we focus our thoughts—and attune our hearts—to the will of God, we will make each day another stage in the spiritual journey . . . and that's precisely what God intends for us to do.

One of the marks of spiritual maturity
is a consistent, Spirit-controlled life.
Vonette Bright

Making Peace with Your Past

The Lord says, "Forget what happened before.
Do not think about the past.
Look at the new thing I am going to do."
Isaiah 43:18–19 ICB

Have you made peace with your past? If so, congratulations. But if you're mired in the quicksand of regret, it's time to plan your escape. How can you do that? By accepting what has been and by trusting God for what will be.

Perhaps you're slow to forget yesterday's disappointments; if so, you're not alone. But if you sincerely want to focus your hopes and energies on the future, you must find ways to accept the past, no matter how difficult it may be.

If you haven't yet made peace with the past, today is the day to declare an end to the hostilities. Then you can turn your thoughts to the wondrous promises of God and to the glorious future He has in store for you.

The past should be culled like a box of fresh
strawberries, rinsed of debris, sweetened judiciously
and served in small portions, not very often.
Laura Palmer

Freedom from the Chains of Perfectionism

Let not your heart be troubled.
John 14:27 KJV

So many expectations! We all know that the demands of everyday living can be high, and the expectations of others can be even higher.

The media delivers an endless stream of messages telling us how to look, how to behave, how to eat, and how to dress. Even our family and friends have expectations of us. And we try hard to meet them. So it's good to stop and remember that God doesn't expect us to be perfect, and neither should we expect perfection from ourselves.

The difference between perfectionism and realistic expectations is the difference between a life of frustration and a life of contentment. God is perfect; we human beings are not. May we live—and forgive—accordingly.

Striving for excellence motivates you;
striving for perfection is demoralizing.
Harriet Braiker

Your Problems, His Opportunities

The LORD has been my defense,
and my God the rock of my refuge.
Psalm 94:22 NKJV

Here's a riddle: What is too unimportant to pray about yet too big for God to handle? The answer is nothing. Yet sometimes, when the challenges of the day seem overwhelming, we may spend more time worrying about our troubles than praying about them. We spend more time fretting about our problems than solving them. A far better strategy, of course, is to pray as if everything depended entirely upon God and to work as if everything depended entirely upon us.

When we learn to see our problems as God sees them—as opportunities for transformation and growth—we begin to change our lives and our world. And the best time to begin that transformation is now.

If you simply let a problem wash around in your mind,
it will seem greater and much more vague
than it will appear on close examination.
Dorothea Brande

Embracing the Simple Life

Proclaim the Message with intensity;
keep on your watch. Challenge, warn, and urge
your people. Don't ever quit. Just keep it simple.
2 Timothy 4:2 MSG

Is yours a life of moderation or accumulation? Are you more interested in the possessions you can acquire or in the person you can become?

Ours is a highly complicated society, a place where people and corporations vie for your attention, for your time, and for your dollars. Don't let them succeed in complicating your life!

If your material possessions are somehow distancing you from God, discard them. If your outside interests leave you too little time for your family, slow down the merry-go-round, or better yet, get off. Simplify your life by stripping away unnecessary possessions and obligations. Simple living is sweet.

For fast-acting relief, try slowing down.
Lily Tomlin

Celebration Time

Rejoice always; pray without ceasing.
1 Thessalonians 5:16–17 NASB

Do you celebrate the gifts God has given you? Do you rejoice in the beauty of God's glorious creation? Do you pray without ceasing? Perhaps, as a busy women living in a demanding world, you've been distracted and drawn away from communing with the Creator.

We're all blessed beyond measure, and we should celebrate our blessings every day. Today is a nonrenewable resource—once it's gone, it's gone forever. Let's give thanks for God's gifts and use those gifts in the service of His people. After all, the blessings we receive from God are multiplied when we share them with others. And that's reason to celebrate!

If you can forgive the person you were,
accept the person you are, and
believe in the person you will become,
you are headed for joy. So celebrate your life.
Barbara Johnson

What's the Big Idea?

With God nothing will be impossible.
Luke 1:37 NKJV

Ruth Handler was a partner in a small business that made plastic items and a few toys. It was a small company called Mattel. But everything changed in 1959 when Ruth observed her daughter Barbara pretending that paper dolls were grownups. That gave Ruth the idea for a grown-up doll she called Barbie in honor of her daughter. Since then over a billion Barbie dolls have been sold—so many that Mattel has lost count.

Ruth is proof that good ideas are everywhere—we can even get them from our kids. So keep your eyes open for a big idea that can change your world. You'll soon discover that new ideas (and fresh opportunities) are like Barbie dolls—too numerous to count.

We must treat ideas somewhat as though they were baby fish. Throw thousands into the waters. Only a handful will survive, but that is plenty.
Anne Hayward

Time Out for a Tune-up

A miserable heart means a miserable life;
a cheerful heart fills the day with song.
Proverbs 15:15 MSG

Life is a cause for celebration, but sometimes we don't feel much like celebrating. In fact, when the weight of the world seems to bear down on our shoulders, celebrating may be the last thing on our minds. But it shouldn't be.

What's your attitude today? Are you pessimistic, perplexed, pained, and perturbed? If so, take a time-out and give your attitude a tune-up.

When you find yourself dwelling on the negative aspects of your life, refocus your attention on the positive things. The next time you're tempted to waste valuable time gossiping or complaining, resist those temptations with all your might.

A life that is free from negativity is yours to claim today.

What lies behind us and what lies before us
are tiny matters compared to what lies within us.
Author Unknown

Embracing the Golden Rule

> *Bear ye one another's burdens,*
> *and so fulfill the law of Christ.*
> Galatians 6:2 KJV

Would you like to make the world a better place and feel better about yourself at the same time? You can start by practicing one of the simplest principles—one we've all heard: the Golden Rule.

The Golden Rule teaches us to treat others in the same way we wish to be treated: with respect, kindness, courtesy, and love. When we do, we make other people happy, we make God happy, and we feel better about ourselves too.

Let the Golden Rule be your guide to changing the world, one person at a time. And if you want to know just how to treat other people, ask the woman you see every time you gaze into the mirror. She'll tell you exactly what to do.

Your heart is happiest when it's beating for others.
Author Unknown

Prioritizing Moment by Moment

What does the Lord require of you?
To act justly and to love mercy
and to walk humbly with your God.
Micah 6:8 NIV

First things first—words that are easy to speak but hard to put into practice. For busy women living in a demanding world, putting first things first can be difficult indeed. After all, people are expecting many things from us!

If you're having trouble prioritizing your day, perhaps you've been trying to organize your life according to your own plans or others' demands, not God's. Far better for everyone involved would be for you to place your daily obligations in the hands of the One who created you. But to do so, you must prioritize your day according to God's will and His wisdom in all matters.

Do you feel overwhelmed or confused? Turn the concerns of this day over to God—prayerfully, earnestly, and moment by moment.

First things first, second things never.
Shirley Conran

The Wisdom to Be Cheerful

A merry heart doeth good like a medicine:
but a broken spirit drieth the bones.
Proverbs 17:22 KJV

Cheerfulness is a gift we give to others and to ourselves. And why shouldn't we be cheerful? We have every reason to honor our God by sharing hugs and smiles with our loved ones.

Yet sometimes even the most courteous among us are beset by fits of ill temper and frustration. During these moments we may not feel like turning our thoughts and prayers to God, but if we seek to gain perspective and peace, to recover our cheerfulness, that's precisely what we must do.

What is the best way to attain the joy God offers you? By giving the Lord what is rightfully His: your heart, your thoughts, and your trust.

When we bring sunshine into the lives of others,
we're warmed by it ourselves. When we spill
a little happiness, it splashes on us.
Barbara Johnson

Facing Fear

The LORD is with me; I will not be afraid.
What can man do to me?
Psalm 118:6 NIV

Do you prefer to face your fears rather than run from them? If so, you will be blessed because of your willingness to live courageously.

When the apostle Paul wrote to his young protégé Timothy, he reminded him that the God they served is a bold God, and God's Spirit empowers His children with boldness also (see 2 Timothy 1:7). Like Timothy, we all face times of uncertainty and fear. And God's message is the same to us today as it was to Timothy: we can live boldly because the Spirit of God resides in us.

Today, as you face the challenges of everyday living, remember that God is with you, and be not afraid.

A ship in port is safe,
but that's not what ships are built for.
Grace Murray Hopper

Love and Commitment

What therefore God hath joined together,
let not man put asunder.
Matthew 19:6 KJV

Sometimes it's easy to be in love—just ask any blissful young couple who recently became engaged. But sometimes love isn't so smooth—just ask any long-married couple who faces health problems, financial difficulties, family tragedy, or any other significant brand of trouble. Yet real love is strong enough to weather these storms because real love isn't a feeling that comes and goes; it's a level of commitment that remains steady and strong, even when times are tough.

Genuine love is more than a feeling; it's a decision to make love endure, no matter what. So if you're married and you want your love to last forever, then you and your spouse must be totally committed to each other. When you are, you can rest assured that the two of you—plus God—can handle anything that comes your way.

There is nothing more lovely in life than the union
of two people whose love for one another has grown
through the years from the small acorn of
passion to a great rooted tree.
Vita Sackville-West

The Joys of a Clear Conscience

*I strive always to keep my conscience
clear before God and man.*
Acts 24:16 NIV

It has been said that character is what we are when nobody is watching. How true. Too often, when we do things that we know aren't right, we try to hide them from our families and friends. But even then God is watching.

Few things in life torment us more than a guilty conscience. And few things in life provide more contentment than the knowledge that we're obeying the conscience God has placed in our hearts.

If you want to create the best possible life for yourself and your loved ones, never forsake your conscience. Remember, when you walk with God, your character will take care of itself. You won't need to look over your shoulder to see who's watching.

There is no pillow so soft as a clear conscience.
Old Saying

Paying Attention

*By wisdom a house is built, and through understanding
it is established; through knowledge its rooms
are filled with rare and beautiful treasures.*
Proverbs 24:3–4 NIV

In the days before her invention, if you wanted
baby food, you had to strain it yourself. And
that's exactly what Dorothy Gerber was doing back
in 1927 when she decided there had to be a better
way. Luckily, her husband's family business produced
canned fruits and vegetables. So when Mrs. Gerber
told her husband, Dan, that baby food would be a hit
with moms, he listened, and the rest is history.

The Gerber story illustrates that great ideas can
be right under our noses. You can make your world
a better place if you keep your eyes open and your
brain in gear.

*That is the way things come clear.
All of a sudden. And then you realize
how obvious they've been all along.*
Madeleine L'Engle

Through the Difficult Days

I will not abandon you as orphans—I will come to you.
John 14:18 NLT

All of us face difficult days. Sometimes even the most optimistic women can become discouraged, and you're no exception. If you find yourself barely enduring your difficult circumstances, perhaps it's time for an extreme intellectual makeover. Perhaps it's time to focus more on your strengths and opportunities, and less on the challenges that confront you. Perhaps it's time to put a little more faith in God.

Your heavenly Father is a God of possibility, not negativity. He will guide you through your difficult days and beyond them. Then, with a renewed spirit of optimism and hope, you'll thank the Giver of all good things for His bountiful gifts.

God never gives up on you,
so don't you ever give up on Him.
Marie T. Freeman

The Courage to Dream Big Dreams

We wait for the LORD; He is our help and shield.
Psalm 33:20 HCSB

Are you willing to entertain the possibility that God has big plans in store for you? It's true. Yet sometimes, especially if you've recently experienced a life-altering disappointment, you may find it difficult to envision a brighter future for yourself and your family. If so, take a second look at your own capabilities—and at God's.

Your heavenly Father created you with unique gifts and talents; your job is to tap into them. When you do, you'll feel an increasing sense of confidence in yourself and in your future.

It takes courage to dream big dreams, but remember that nothing is too difficult for God, and no dreams are too big for Him—not even yours. So start living—and dreaming—accordingly.

If you doubt you can accomplish something,
you can't accomplish it. Instead, you have to be
confident in yourself, and you need to be
tough enough to follow through.
Rosalynn Carter

Get Excited!

Rejoice in the Lord . . . again I say, Rejoice.
Philippians 4:4 KJV

Are you burning with enthusiasm about your life, your friends, your family, and your future? If so, congratulations and keep up the good work! But if your spiritual batteries are running low, perhaps you're spending too much energy focusing on your losses and too little time planning for future victories.

Writer Sara Jordan gave this simple but good advice: "Every day give yourself a good mental shampoo."

If you're feeling tired or troubled or both, take time to soak in your blessings as you focus on things that are positive. And while you're at it, seek strength from the Source that never fails. When you sincerely petition God, He will give you all the power and enthusiasm you need to live victoriously through Him.

Success is a state of mind. If you want success,
start thinking of yourself as a success.
Joyce Brothers

Faith That Moves Mountains

If you have faith as small as a mustard seed, you can say to this mountain, "Move from here to there" and it will move. Nothing will be impossible for you.
Matthew 17:20 NIV

Have you ever felt your faith in God slipping away? You are not alone. Every life—including yours—is a series of successes and failures, celebrations and disappointments, joys and sorrows. But even when we feel distant from God, God is never distant from us.

Faith can move mountains. When you place your faith, your trust, indeed your life in the hands of God, you'll be amazed at the marvelous things He can do with you and through you. So strengthen your faith through praise, through worship, and through prayer, and trust God's plans. With Him all things are possible, and He stands ready to open a world of possibilities to you if you'll just have a little faith.

Faith in faith is pointless. Faith in a living, active God moves mountains.
Beth Moore

Time for Family

*Unless the LORD builds the house, they labor in vain
who build it; unless the LORD guards the city, the
watchman stays awake in vain.*
Psalm 127:1 NKJV

Caring for your family requires time—lots of time.
You've probably heard about "quality time" and
"quantity time." Your family needs both, and you
willingly invest large quantities of your time and
energy in the care and nurturing of your clan.

Still, these are difficult days for every household:
never have distractions and temptations been greater.
Thankfully, God is bigger than all those challenges.
So while you're caring for your family, do your best
to ensure that God remains squarely at the center
of your family life. When you do, God will bless you
and yours in ways you haven't even imagined.

*The miraculous thing about being a family is that
in the last analysis, we are each dependent on
one another and God, woven together
by mercy given and mercy received.*
Barbara Johnson

November

November 1

Your Body, God's Temple

*Whatever you eat or drink or whatever you do,
you must do all for the glory of God.*
1 Corinthians 10:31 NLT

Are you shaping up or spreading out? Do you eat sensibly and exercise regularly, or do you spend most of your time on the couch thinking about exercising regularly? Are you treating your body like the temple it is? How you answer these questions will help determine how long and how well you live.

Your body is God's temple, an amazing creation that deserves first-class treatment. Physical fitness is a choice, and it requires discipline—it's as simple as that.

Starting today, do yourself and your loved ones this favor: treat your body like a one-of-a-kind gift from God—because that's precisely what it is.

*Our primary motivation should not be for
more energy or to avoid a heart attack
but to please God with our bodies.*
Carole Lewis

Finding Fulfillment

*Ask and you will receive, so that
your joy will be the fullest possible joy.*
John 16:24 NCV

Everywhere we turn, or so it seems, the world promises fulfillment, contentment, and happiness. But the contentment the world offers is fleeting and incomplete. Thankfully, the fulfillment God offers is all-encompassing and everlasting.

Sometimes, amid the inevitable hustle and bustle of daily living, we can lose sight of the real joys of life as we wrestle with the challenges that confront us. Yet fulfillment is available to people who seek it in proper places and in proper ways.

The thoughts you think, the actions you take, the prayers you pray, and the people you help largely determine your fulfillment.

If you want to find fulfillment, you have to choose happiness on a daily basis . . . starting now and ending never.

*You are the only person alive
who has sole custody of your life.*
Anna Quindlen

A Willingness to Help

Give to everyone who asks you, and if anyone takes what belongs to you, do not demand it back.
Luke 6:30 NIV

We are to be generous with our friends, with our families, and with those in need. We must give freely of our time, our possessions, and especially our love. And we can do this because we have also freely received all of these things from our heavenly Father.

The apostle Paul taught that when we sow the seeds of generosity, we reap bountiful rewards. But Paul also offered a word of caution: we are to be cheerful givers—not to give "grudgingly or under compulsion" (2 Corinthians 9:7 NASB).

Today find some way to be a cheerful, generous, courageous giver. The world needs your help, and you'll love the spiritual rewards that will be yours when you give it.

A cheerful giver does not count the cost of what he gives. His heart is set on pleasing and cheering him to whom the gift is given.
Julian of Norwich

His Comforting Hand

God, who comforts the downcast, comforted us.
2 Corinthians 7:6 NIV

Even if you are a joyous, optimistic woman, you may find your spirit almost broken by the disappointments and tragedies that are the inevitable consequence of living long and loving deeply. But your heartache need never be in vain.

Elisabeth Kübler-Ross described her own losses this way: "I shall be richer all my life for this sorrow."

On a similar note, singer Judy Collins observed, "Grief shows us the beauties in life and teaches us to appreciate them."

So the next time you find your courage pushed to the limit, lean on God's promises and accept the touch of His comforting hand. Remember that God rules both on mountaintops and in valleys, with limitless wisdom and love, now and forever.

Put your hand into the hand of God.
He gives the calmness and serenity of heart and soul.
Mrs. Charles E. Cowman

Life on Your Terms

*Teach us to number our days carefully
so that we may develop wisdom in our hearts.*
Psalm 90:12 HCSB

American novelist Marjorie Kinnan Rawlings was born in Washington, D.C. Forty-two years later her novel *The Yearling* won the Pulitzer Prize. Marjorie always placed a high value on individuality, once observing, "It is more important to live the life one wishes to live and to go down with it, if necessary, than live more profitably but less happily."

At times society will attempt to pigeonhole you, to standardize you, to make you fit into a particular, preformed mold. But perhaps God has other plans—and perhaps you do too. So when in doubt, be yourself. The world loves an original, and when it comes to being you, absolutely no one is more qualified.

*Life loves to be taken by the lapel and told,
"I am with you kid. Let's go."*
Maya Angelou

It's a Wonderful Life

*Flee from youthful passions, and pursue
righteousness, faith, love, and peace.*
2 Timothy 2:22 HCSB

Donna Mullenger was discovered in Hollywood, changed her name, and began a movie career. She played the role of Mary Bailey in the holiday favorite *It's a Wonderful Life*. But her greatest fame came as the star of the show that bore her name, *The Donna Reed Show*. On TV she played the perfect mom. Behind the scenes Donna was also a hardworking creative force and a TV pioneer.

Another TV mom, Lucille Ball, said: "I don't trust luck. Luck is really just hard work and realizing what your opportunities are and aren't."

Lucy was right. And when you realize the opportunities you have to show love, do what is right, and trust God, it really can be a wonderful life.

*I wish to live because life has with it that which is good,
that which is beautiful, and that which is love.*
Lorraine Hansberry

Making a Difference

Learn to do right! Seek justice, encourage the oppressed.
Isaiah 1:17 NIV

Years ago the Florida Everglades was considered a wasteland. The mood of the public seemed to be, "Drain the swamp!" But in 1947 a naturalist named Marjory Stoneman Douglas changed all that. Her book, called *The Everglades: River of Grass*, pointed out that the Everglades was not a swampy wasteland but rather a shallow river flowing through a grassy plain. Largely because of Marjory's work, the Everglades was declared a national park, preserving it for generations to come.

One woman can make a difference. So the next time you feel swamped by a big challenge, remember the writer who made history in the Everglades. Then get busy and start making some history of your own.

Our lives, we are told, are but fleeting at best,
Like roses they fade and decay;
Then let us do good while the present is ours,
Be useful as long as we stay.
Fanny Crosby

Neighbors in Need

*Above all these things put on charity,
which is the bond of perfectness.*
Colossians 3:14 KJV

We know that we are instructed to love our neighbors, and yet there's so little time, and we're so busy. No matter. We are to love them just as we love ourselves. In order to love our neighbors as God intends, we must first slow down long enough to understand their needs. Slowing down, however, is not as simple as it seems.

We live in a fast-paced world with pressures and demands that often sap our time and our energy. Sometimes we may convince ourselves that slowing down is not an option, but we're wrong. Caring for our neighbors must be our priority because it is God's priority.

If you don't love those around you, who will? Today look for a neighbor in need . . . and then do something to help. Father's orders.

*We can't help everyone,
but everyone can help someone.*
Loretta Scott

November 9

Embracing Truth

*You shall know the truth,
and the truth shall make you free.*

John 8:32 NKJV

These words from the Gospel of John are both familiar and straightforward—the truth, indeed, sets us free. Yet we live in a world that not only allows but actually encourages us to overlook the truth (or to deny it altogether).

Best-selling author M. Scott Peck said, "Truth or reality is avoided when it is painful. Mental health is an ongoing process of dedication to reality at all costs."

According to philosopher Eric Hopper, "We lie loudest when we lie to ourselves."

Today, as you fulfill the responsibilities God has placed before you, ask yourself this question: do my thoughts and actions bear witness to the ultimate truth God has placed in my heart, or am I allowing the pressures of everyday life to overwhelm me? It's a profound question that deserves an answer.

*The easiest things to ignore are
the things we don't want to see.*

Marie T. Freeman

God's Lessons

*Start with God—the first step in learning
is bowing down to God.*
Proverbs 1:7 MSG

When it comes to life's lessons, we can learn them the easy way, or we can learn them the hard way. The easy way can be summed up as follows: when God teaches us a lesson, we learn it—the first time. Unfortunately, too many of us catch on much more slowly than that.

When we resist God's instruction, He continues to teach us, whether we like it or not. Our challenge, then, is to discern God's lessons from the experiences of everyday life. Hopefully, we learn those lessons sooner rather than later—because the sooner we do, the sooner our heavenly Father can move on to the next lesson, and the next, and the next . . .

*True learning can take place at every age of life,
and it doesn't have to be in the curriculum plan.*
Suzanne Dale Ezell

Go for the Gold

*Each person should examine his own work,
and then he will have a reason for boasting in himself
alone, and not in respect to someone else.
For each person will have to carry his own load.*
Galatians 6:4–5 HCSB

In 1984 no American female gymnast had ever won an individual Olympic medal. But Mary Lou Retton changed all that when she won five medals, including a gold. Her accomplishments were even more amazing because they came only two months after surgery on her knee. Looking back on her intensive preparation, Mary Lou said, "Working hard became a habit, a serious kind of fun."

Even if you don't know the difference between a pommel horse and a charley horse, you can still take a lesson from the then ninety-eight-pound bundle of energy who took the world of gymnastics by storm. If you make the work fun, there's no limit to the things you can accomplish. Today look for ways to make your job a pleasure, not a punishment. When you do, you'll give a winning performance.

*No matter how far a person can go,
the horizon is still way beyond you.*
Zora Neale Hurston

The Wisdom of Positive Thinking

I can do everything through him who gives me strength.
Philippians 4:13 NIV

Women have every reason to be optimistic about life here on earth and life eternal. Sometimes, despite our trust in God, we still may fall into the spiritual quagmire of worry, frustration, anxiety, or sheer exhaustion, and our hearts become heavy. What's needed is plenty of rest, a large dose of perspective, and God's healing touch—but not necessarily in that order.

Today vow to be a hope-filled woman. Think optimistically about your life, your profession, and your future. Then, when you've filled your heart with hope, share your optimism and gladness with a world that needs both.

Optimism is that faith that leads to achievement.
Nothing can be done without hope and confidence.
Helen Keller

With God's Strength

Search for the Lord and for His strength;
seek His face always.
Psalm 105:4 HCSB

As you continually seek God's purpose for your life, you will undoubtedly experience your fair share of disappointments, detours, false starts, and failures. When you do, don't become discouraged; God's not finished with you yet.

The saying is as true today as it was when it was first spoken: "Life is a marathon, not a sprint." That's why wise life travelers select a traveling companion who never tires and never falters. That partner is your heavenly Father.

Are you tired? Ask God for strength. Are you discouraged? Believe in His promises. Do you feel defeated? Pray for the ultimate victory that is sure to come. Have faith that you are destined to play an important role in God's great plan for humankind— because you do.

We ought to make some progress, however little,
every day, and show some increase of fervor.
We ought to act as if we were at war—
as, indeed, we are—and never relax
until we have won the victory.
Saint Teresa of Avila

Do It Now

*If you make a promise to God, don't be slow
to keep it. God is not happy with fools,
so give God what you promised.*
Ecclesiastes 5:4 NCV

The habit of procrastination takes a twofold toll on its victims. First, important work goes unfinished; second, valuable energy is wasted in the process of putting off the things that remain undone. Procrastination results from an individual's short-sighted attempt to postpone temporary discomfort. What results is a senseless cycle of delay followed by worry followed by a panicky and often futile attempt to catch up. Procrastination is, at its core, a struggle against oneself—and the only antidote is action.

Once you acquire the habit of doing what needs to be done when it needs to be done, you'll avoid untold trouble and stress. God has created a world that rewards those who "do it now." In other words, life doesn't procrastinate. Neither should you.

*All that is necessary to break the spell of inertia and
frustration is this: act as if it were impossible to fail.
That is the talisman, the formula,
the command of right-about-face which
turns us from failure towards success.*
Dorothea Brande

Demonstrating Our Beliefs

Be not faithless, but believing.
John 20:27 KJV

When it comes to beliefs, our actions are far better indicators than our words. Yet far too many of us spend more energy talking about our beliefs than living by them—with predictable consequences.

Is your life a picture book of your creed? Are your actions congruent with your beliefs? Are you willing to practice the philosophies you preach? If so, you are a powerful example to your family and friends.

Each day presents a fresh opportunity to make certain that your actions are guided by the conscience God has given you. So don't treat your faith as if it were separate from your everyday life. Weave your beliefs into the very fabric of your day. When you do, God will honor your good works, and your good works will honor God.

Strong convictions precede great actions.
Author Unknown

Living and Learning

*There's something here also for seasoned men and
women, still a thing or two for the experienced to
learn—fresh wisdom to probe and penetrate,
the rhymes and reasons of wise
men and women. Start with God.*

Proverbs 1:5–7 MSG

Actress Tallulah Bankhead, whose father was a
U.S. Congressman and Speaker of the House,
was bothered as a child by bronchial ailments that
deepened her voice, giving it a smoky quality that
would become her signature. When Tallulah made
her Broadway debut in 1918, she began a career that
would span five decades.

Ms. Bankhead once offhandedly remarked, "If I
had my life to live over, I'd make the same mistakes,
only sooner." Mistakes are life's practical instructors,
without which we might never learn much about
anything. All experiences, both good and bad, have
the power to instruct. It's up to us to make certain
that whenever our mistakes have lessons to teach,
we have the good sense to be taught.

*Learning is not attained by chance; it must be sought
for with ardor and attended to with diligence.*

Abigail Adams

Forgiveness at Home

*If anyone says, "I am living in the light,"
but hates a Christian brother or sister,
that person is still living in darkness.*
1 John 2:9 NLT

Sometimes it's easy to become angry with the people we love most—and sometimes it's hard to forgive them. After all, we know that our family will still love us no matter how angry we become. But while it's easy to get angry at home, it's usually wrong.

Because no family is perfect, no family is totally free of squabbles, disagreements, misunderstandings, and hurt feelings. But family arguments should never be allowed to fester; they should be addressed and resolved, however difficult that resolution may be.

The next time you're tempted to stay angry at a husband, a child, a sibling, or a parent, remember that these are the people who love you more than anyone else. Then calm down and forgive them—because peace is always beautiful, especially when it's peace at your house.

Home is where I know true peace and love.
Anita Baker

The Balancing Act Called Life

I place before you Life and Death, Blessing and Curse.
Choose life so that you and your children will live.
Deuteronomy 30:19 MSG

Face facts: life is a delicate balancing act, a tightrope walk with over-commitment on one side and under-commitment on the other. And it's up to each of us to walk carefully on that rope, not falling prey to pride (which causes us to attempt too much) or to fear (which causes us to attempt too little).

God's Word promises us the possibility of abundance (see John 10:10). And we are far more likely to experience that abundance when we lead balanced lives.

Are you doing too much—or too little? If so, it's time to have a little chat with God. And if you listen carefully to His instructions, you will strive to achieve a more balanced life, a life that's right for you and your loved ones. When you do, everybody wins.

Doing too much is as dangerous as doing nothing at all. Both modes prevent us from savoring our moments. One causes me to rush right past the best of life without recognizing or basking in it, and the other finds me sitting quietly as life rushes past me.
Patsy Clairmont

A Practical Theology

*Be ye doers of the word, and not hearers only,
deceiving your own selves.*
James 1:22 KJV

We must do our best to ensure that we are practical people, quick to act whenever we see an opportunity to serve God.

Are you the kind of person who is willing to dig in and do what needs to be done when it needs to be done? If so, congratulations. God acknowledges your service and blesses it. But if you ever find yourself more interested in the fine points of theology than in the needs of your neighbors, perhaps it's time for a second look at your priorities.

Theology is a good thing until it interferes with God's work. It's up to you to make sure your theology doesn't. God needs people who are willing to roll up their sleeves and go to work for Him. Count yourself among that number.

Deeds, not creeds, are the measure of a person.
Author Unknown

You Are Blessed

The LORD is good, and His love is eternal;
His faithfulness endures through all generations.
Psalm 100:5 HCSB

Do you know how richly you have been blessed? While God's gifts are too numerous to count, you'll be wise to inventory as many blessings as you can, as often as you can.

Author Elisabeth Elliot said, "It is always possible to be thankful for what is given rather than to complain about what is not given. One or the other becomes a habit of life."

Remember, as songwriter Gloria Gaither encourages us, "God has promised that if we harvest well with the tools of thanksgiving, there will be seeds for planting in the spring."

Are you taking God's gifts for granted? That would be a disservice to your Creator and to yourself. The best way to resolve that problem is to make every day a time for celebration and praise. Starting today.

If you pause to think—you'll have cause to thank!
Author Unknown

A Glass Half Full

Make me hear joy and gladness.
Psalm 51:8 NKJV

As you look at the landscape of your life, do you see opportunities, possibilities, and blessings, or do you focus instead on the less pleasant scenery? Do you spend more time counting your blessings or your misfortunes? If you've acquired the unfortunate habit of focusing too intently on the negative aspects of life, then your spiritual vision is in need of correction.

Today is yet another gift from God, and it presents yet another opportunity to thank Him for His gifts. If you're wise, you'll give thanks early and often.

The way you choose to view the scenery around you will have a profound impact on the quality, the tone, and the direction of your life. The more you focus on the beauty that surrounds you, the more beautiful your own life will become.

If you can't tell whether your glass is half-empty
or half-full, you don't need another glass;
what you need is better eyesight . . .
and a more thankful heart.
Marie T. Freeman

Doing What You Can

The LORD is my light and my salvation;
whom shall I fear? The LORD is the strength
of my life; of whom shall I be afraid?
Psalm 27:1 KJV

The year was 1955, and a seamstress named Rosa Parks was riding a bus in Montgomery, Alabama. In those days African-Americans were required to give up their seats to whites. But Rosa refused—so she was arrested. Her personal protest against injustice ignited the civil-rights movement in the United States. Rosa's philosophy was powerfully simple: "I don't waste too much time thinking about my problems. I just look around to see what I can do, and then I do it."

If you've been thinking you can't make changes in your world, think again. Remember Rosa Parks, and summon the courage to make big changes in your own life and in your world. Rosa did it, and so can you.

God is voting for us all the time.
The devil is voting against us all the time.
The way we vote carries the election.
Corrie ten Boom

Hugs of Compassion

*All of you should be of one mind, full of sympathy
toward each other, loving one another
with tender hearts and humble minds.*
1 Peter 3:8 NLT

God commands us to be compassionate and generous to those who need support. We have been richly blessed by our Creator, and we in turn are asked to share our gifts, our possessions, and our talents.

Concentration-camp survivor Corrie ten Boom said, "The measure of a life is not its duration but its donation." Her words remind us that the quality of our lives is determined not by what we're able to take from others but by what we are able to share with them.

The thread of compassion is woven into the very fabric of all of God's teachings. We must be zealous in caring for others. In light of His love and compassion for us, how can we do less?

*Before you can dry another's tears,
you too must weep.*
Barbara Johnson

Content with Who You Are

*You're blessed when you're content with
just who you are—no more, no less.
That's the moment you find yourselves proud
owners of everything that can't be bought.*
Matthew 5:5 MSG

In 1922 Frances Ethel Gumm was born. Frances changed her name to Judy Garland at the insistence of well-known entertainer George Jessel while performing with his act during the 1934 World's Fair in Chicago. After moving to Hollywood with her family, Judy signed a movie contract with MGM in 1935 (she was only thirteen at the time). Garland made thirty-two feature films, the most notable of which was *The Wizard of Oz*.

Judy gave this straightforward advice: "Always be a first-rate version of yourself instead of a second-rate version of someone else."

It's tempting to go along with the crowd, but the crowd may not be going in your direction. So copy no one—make up your mind to be the real you. Be content knowing that you are a unique woman created by a loving God.

*Faith in God is the greatest power . . .
but great, too, is faith in oneself.*
Mary McLeod Bethune

Expect the Best

> *We are hoping for something we do not have yet,*
> *and we are waiting for it patiently.*
> Romans 8:25 NCV

Born in 1850, Ella Wheeler Wilcox wrote daily poems for a syndicate of newspapers. Later, more than twenty volumes of her verse were published. In a poem titled "Optimism," Ella wrote, "Say that you are well and all is well with you, and God will hear your words and make them true."

The self-fulfilling prophecy is a reality. If you constantly anticipate the worst, that's what you're likely to attract. But if you make the effort to think positive thoughts, those thoughts might just come true.

So put the self-fulfilling prophecy to work for you—expect the best and you'll immediately increase your chances of achieving the best.

> *Treat people as if they were what they*
> *ought to be and you help them to become*
> *what they are capable of being.*
> Johann Wolfgang von Goethe

Those Who Persevere

*Endurance must do its complete work, so that
you may be mature and complete, lacking nothing.*
James 1:4 HCSB

Sometimes it's tempting to give up at the first
sign of trouble. Tempting but wrong. Why?
Because God has work for you to do—important
work. And He's given you an impressive array of
talents and opportunities with which to accomplish
the work at hand.

When it comes to your particular genius—and
you can be quite sure that you have one—it's your
job to transform potential into reality. Making
your dreams come true is largely up to you. What's
required is perseverance.

The next time you're tempted to give up on
your big dream, remember the words of Margaret
Thatcher, who said, "You may have to fight a battle
more than once to win it." Keep fighting for your
dreams until you make them come true!

*Every action we take, everything we do,
is either a victory or defeat in
the struggle to become what we want to be.*
Anne Byrhhe

Your Very Bright Future

*Be of good courage, and He shall strengthen your heart,
all you who hope in the LORD.*

Psalm 31:24 NKJV

Do you expect your future to be bright? Are you willing to dream king-sized dreams and to work diligently to make those dreams happen?

God promises that we can do all things through Him. Yet most of us live far below our potential. We take half measures; we dream small dreams; we waste precious time and energy on the distractions of the world. But God has better plans for us.

In her diary Anne Frank wrote, "The good news is that you really don't know how great you can be, how much you can love, what you can accomplish, and what your potential is." These words apply to you. You possess great potential, potential you must use or forfeit. And the time to claim your very bright future is now.

*You pay God a compliment
by asking great things of Him.*

Saint Teresa of Avila

An Example That Honors God

You are the light that gives light to the world. . . .
In the same way, you should be a light for other people.
Live so that they will see the good things you do
and will praise your Father in heaven.
Matthew 5:14, 16 NCV

Our words speak, but our actions speak much more loudly. So whether we like it or not, all of us are role models. Since our friends and family members are always observing our actions, we inevitably influence the way they behave by the way we behave.

Well-known evangelist Dwight L. Moody once said, "It is a great deal better to live a holy life than to talk about it. Lighthouses do not ring bells and fire cannons to call attention to their shining—they just shine."

The world needs women like you who are willing to stand up and be counted as positive role models. Your family and friends are watching you, and so is God. And He will reward your willingness to be the right kind of example.

We are to leave an impression on all those
we meet that communicates whose we are
and what kingdom we represent.
Lisa Bevere

November 29

Temporary Setbacks

*Sometimes I ask God, my rock-solid God,
"Why did you let me down? Why am I walking
around in tears, harassed by enemies?"*
Psalm 42:9 MSG

Occasional disappointments and failures in life are inevitable. They're simply the price that we must pay for our willingness to take risks as we follow our dreams. But even when we encounter setbacks, we must never lose faith.

American children's rights advocate Marian Wright Edelman asked, "Whoever said anybody has a right to give up?" That's a question you should ask yourself, especially when times get tough.

Are you willing to keep fighting the good fight even when you meet unexpected difficulties? If you'll decide to press on through temporary setbacks, you may soon be surprised at the creative ways God finds to help determined people like you—people who possess the wisdom and the courage to persevere.

A fall is not a signal to lie wallowing, but to rise.
Christina Rossetti

Lots to Learn

Commit yourself to instruction;
attune your ears to hear words of knowledge.
Proverbs 23:12 NLT

Whether you're twenty-five or ninety-five, you still have lots to learn—and that's good! The world is an exciting place for thoughtful people like you who continue to feed their brains a steady supply of good thoughts and new thoughts.

Education is the means by which we come to know and appreciate the world. Learning is not a luxury, it's a necessity and a powerful tool for good in this world. And it's a tool we should use—and share—during every stage of life. Eleanor Roosevelt noted, "All of life is a constant education."

One sure benefit of education, as teacher Marva Collins pointed out, is that "when someone is taught the joy of learning, it becomes a lifelong process that never stops."

Lifetime learning is both wonderful and essential. Class is never really dismissed.

Real education should educate us out of self
and into something far finer; into a selflessness
which links us with all humanity.
Nancy Astor

December

Decision Making 101

> *Don't abandon wisdom, and she will watch over you;*
> *love her, and she will guard you.*
> Proverbs 4:6 HCSB

Are you facing a difficult decision, a troubling circumstance, or a powerful temptation? If so, maybe it's time to step back, stop focusing on what others want you to do, and focus instead on what your conscience tells you to do.

Life is an exercise in decision making. Today and every day, you must make choices: choices about what you will do, what you will worship, and how you will think. When in doubt, make wise choices that you sincerely believe will bring you into a closer relationship with God. And if you're uncertain of your next step, slow down long enough to pray about it. When you do, answers will come. And you can rest assured that when God answers prayer, His answers are the right ones for you.

> *The Old Testament prophets did not say,*
> *"Brothers, I want a consensus."*
> Margaret Thatcher

A Fresh Supply of Hope

Each generation can set its hope anew on God,
remembering his glorious miracles
and obeying his commands.
Psalm 78:7 NLT

Today you have every reason to rejoice. After all, God remains in His heaven, and the sun has risen on another day of life. But when the demands of living seem great, you may find yourself struggling to rejoice; you may feel exhausted and discouraged. That's when you need a fresh supply of hope—and God is ready, willing, and able to supply it.

The advice in Proverbs 4:25 is clear-cut: "Keep your eyes focused on what is right, and look straight ahead to what is good" (NCV). Strive to maintain a positive, can-do attitude—an expectant attitude that lifts your own spirits and the spirits of your friends and neighbors.

As you face the challenges of the coming day, ask God for another daily dose of hope. When you ask sincerely, you will receive.

Worry does not empty tomorrow of its sorrow;
it empties today of its strength.
Corrie ten Boom

A Work of Love

These things I have spoken to you, that My joy may remain in you, and that your joy may be full.
John 15:11 NKJV

Gracie Allen married George Burns in 1926, and the two formed one of America's most popular comedy teams. Gracie played the role of the confused, linguistically challenged wife, while George played the role of the loving but frustrated husband.

Gracie died in 1964, but George lived until 1996, becoming one of America's most beloved senior citizens. The George Burns secret to success was simple. He said, "My best advice is this: fall in love with what you do for a living."

Have you found work that fits your personality and makes the world a better place? If so, you are richly blessed. If not, keep searching, because the world needs your best work—and you will surely enjoy finding it.

As long as I can work, I'm happy.
Lucille Ball

Your Way or God's Way

Each of us will have to answer to God.
Romans 14:12 NCV

The popular song "My Way" is a perfectly good tune, but it's not such a great guide for living. If you're looking for life's perfect prescription, forget about insisting on your own way and start doing things God's way, even if you're sorely tempted to do otherwise.

Sometimes God's plans are crystal clear to us; sometimes they're not. When you're uncertain about God's direction for your life, keep searching and keep praying. If you do, in time God will answer your prayers and make His plans known. You'll discover His plans by doing things His way, and you'll be eternally grateful that you did.

God not only orders our steps but He orders our stops.
Author Unknown

Courtesy Matters

*Dear friend, when you extend hospitality to
Christian brothers and sisters, even when
they are strangers, you make the faith visible.*
3 John 1:5 MSG

Even in a culturally diverse world, some matters of etiquette and courtesy are universal. Matthew 7:12 says, "In everything, therefore, treat people the same way you want them to treat you" (NASB).

God's instructions aren't, "In some things treat people as you wish to be treated." He doesn't say, "From time to time treat others with kindness." God wants us to treat others as we wish to be treated in every aspect of our daily lives.

Today try to be a little kinder than necessary to family members, friends, and total strangers. And as you consider all the things God has done for you, honor Him with your kind words and good deeds. He deserves no less, and neither do your loved ones.

*Small kindnesses, small courtesies, small considerations,
habitually practiced in our social intercourse,
give a greater charm to the character than
the display of great talents and accomplishments.*
Mary Ann Kelty

Rewarded by the Work

Hard work means prosperity;
only fools idle away their time.
Proverbs 12:11 NLT

Oprah Winfrey's father is Vernon Winfrey, the proprietor of Vernon Winfrey's Barber Shop on Vernon Winfrey Boulevard in Nashville, Tennessee.

As a young man Vernon plowed Mississippi cotton fields behind a mule. Today, despite his daughter's urgings to retire, Winfrey continues to do what he's done for many years: cut hair. Why? Because he loves his work, and he loves his customers.

All of us should strive to be like Vernon Winfrey; we should search for meaningful work, work that we love, work that we're anxious to do. That kind of work is its own reward, and when we find it, we're sure to make the cut.

If you always do what interests you,
at least one person will be pleased.
Katharine Hepburn

Sisters, Friends

Love from the center of who you are;
don't fake it. Run for dear life from evil;
hold on for dear life to good.
Romans 12:9 MSG

They were sisters and they were best friends. They were the incomparable centenarians, the Delaney sisters. When Bessie and Sadie Delaney published their memoirs in 1993, American readers rejoiced at the wit and wisdom of two women who had shared a hundred years together. Bessie Delaney was the second African-American woman to be licensed to practice dentistry in New York. Sadie was the first black woman to teach domestic science in a New York high school. Both women were opinionated, insightful, and enthusiastic about life.

The Delaney sisters understood the importance of family and the importance of friendship. And they both understood (from personal experience) that a beloved family member and a best friend are often one and the same.

A genuine friendship is a heavenly present.
It blesses our hearts because God's love is in it.
Evelyn McCurdy

Answering the Call

*As God has distributed to each one,
as the Lord has called each one, so let him walk.*
1 Corinthians 7:17 NKJV

It is terribly important that you heed God's calling by discovering and developing the talents He has given you. If you want to make a difference in the world around you and in the lives of your family and friends, you must discover your gifts and begin using them today—not tomorrow or at some distant time in the future.

Author Barbara Johnson spoke for women of every generation when she said, "We are all on our way somewhere. We'll get there if we just keep going."

Every person on earth possesses at least one important gift. Have you found your special calling? If not, keep searching until you find it. God has important work for you to do, and the time to begin that work is now.

*If God has called you,
do not spend time looking over your shoulder
to see who is following you.*
Corrie ten Boom

Too Much of a Good Thing

A devout life does bring wealth, but it's the rich
simplicity of being yourself before God.
Since we entered the world penniless and
will leave it penniless, if we have bread
on the table and shoes on our feet, that's enough.
1 Timothy 6:6–8 MSG

Do you sometimes feel swamped by your stuff? Do you find yourself spending more and more time keeping track of the things you own while making mental notes of the things you intend to buy? If so, here's a word of warning: your fondness for material possessions may be getting in the way of your relationships—your relationships with the people around you and your relationship with God.

Face facts: material possessions are highly overrated, but you certainly wouldn't know it by strolling through the local mall.

Society teaches us to honor possessions; God teaches us to honor people. Earthly riches are here today and all too soon gone. Our real riches are in heaven, and that's where we should focus our thoughts and our energy.

She who dies with the most toys . . . still dies.
Author Unknown

Your Positive Path

*In all your ways acknowledge Him,
and He shall direct your paths.*
Proverbs 3:6 NKJV

Today you will take one more step on your life's journey. Today offers one more opportunity to be genuinely thankful for your blessings. The coming day is a canvas upon which you can compose a beautiful work of art, and that's precisely what you should do.

Norman Vincent Peale shared this insight: "The life of stress is difficult. But the life of thanksgiving—a life that comes from a positive attitude—is the easiest type of existence."

Today make certain your path is a positive path. When you do, you'll be a genuine blessing to your loved ones and a source of encouragement to a world that desperately needs positive influences such as yours.

*Pessimism is an investment in nothing.
Optimism is an investment in hope.*
Author Unknown

Claiming the Joy

Rejoice evermore. . . . In every thing give thanks:
for this is the will of God.
1 Thessalonians 5:16, 18 KJV

Joni Eareckson Tada spoke for Christian women of every generation when she observed, "I wanted the deepest part of me to vibrate with that ancient yet familiar longing—that desire for something that would fill and overflow my soul."

God's plan for our lives includes great joy, but our heavenly Father will not force His joy upon us. We must accept His peace on our own—no one can accept it for us.

Today let's claim the joy God has provided for us by praising the Creator for the gift of life. Then let's share His love and His joy. When we do, we'll be blessed, and so will our families, our friends, and all whom God has chosen to place along our paths.

Every morning is a fresh opportunity to find
God's extraordinary joy in the most ordinary places.
Janet L. Weaver

Finding a Quiet Place

In quietness and in confidence shall be your strength.
Isaiah 30:15 KJV

The world seems to grow louder day by day, and our senses seem to be invaded at every turn. If we allow the distractions of a clamorous society to separate us from God's peace, we do ourselves a profound disservice. Our task is to carve out moments of silence in a world filled with noise.

If we are to maintain righteous minds and compassionate hearts, we must take time each day for silence and meditation. We must quiet our minds and our hearts so we can sense God's will and His eternal love.

Nothing is more important than the time we spend with our heavenly Father. Today find time to be still and claim the inner peace that is found in the silent moments we spend alone with God.

One needs occasionally to stand aside from the hum and rush of human interests and passions to hear the voice of God.
Anna Julia Cooper

Too Many Temptations

Don't let evil get the best of you;
get the best of evil by doing good.
Romans 12:21 MSG

Because our world is filled with temptations, we confront them at every turn. Some of these temptations are small—eating a second piece of chocolate cake, for example. Too much cake may not be good for the bodies God has entrusted to our care. But two pieces of cake will not bring us to our knees. Other temptations, however, are not so benign.

Your body is a marvelous creation. Your task, as a thoughtful woman, is to treat your body with the care it deserves.

Today you will be tempted to do things that are detrimental to your physical, emotional, or spiritual health. One of the best ways to beat the temptation is to counter it with some positive action. When you do, you'll show that you are wise—and you'll be blessed.

Do not fight the temptation in detail.
Turn from it. Look only at your Lord.
Sing. Read. Work.
Amy Carmichael

Known by Our Actions

Even a child is known by his actions,
by whether his conduct is pure and right.
Proverbs 20:11 NIV

We must do our best to make sure our actions are accurate reflections of our beliefs. Our theology must be demonstrated not only by our words but, more importantly, by our actions. In short, we should be practical, quick to act on the beliefs we hold most dear.

We may proclaim our beliefs to our hearts' content, but our proclamations will mean nothing—to others or to ourselves—unless we accompany our words with deeds that match. The sermons we live are far more compelling than the ones we preach.

Like it or not, your life is an accurate reflection of your creed. If this fact gives you cause for concern, don't bother talking about the changes you intend to make—make them.

Although God causes all things to
work together for good for His children,
He still holds us accountable for our behavior.
Kay Arthur

Turning Away from Anger

A person with great anger bears the penalty.
Proverbs 19:19 HCSB

The frustrations of everyday living can sometimes get the better of us, and we allow minor disappointments to cause us major problems. When we allow ourselves to become overly irritated by the inevitable ups and downs of life, we become overstressed, overheated, overanxious, and just plain angry.

As singer Tina Turner once observed, "If you want to be successful, you don't have time for bitterness." The same can be said about anger.

As the old saying goes, "Anger usually improves nothing but the arch of a cat's back." Don't allow anger to rule your life, or, for that matter, your day—your life is simply too short for that . . . and so is your day.

You cannot shake hands with a clenched fist.
Indira Gandhi

Beyond the Fear of Rejection

*If you're not welcomed, not listened to,
quietly withdraw. Don't make a scene.
Shrug your shoulders and be on your way.*
Mark 6:11 MSG

The fear of rejection and its first cousin, the fear of failure, are roadblocks on the road to happiness. When we try to please everyone in sight, we create for ourselves a goal that is unrealistic, unsatisfying, and unworthy of our efforts.

Children's author Judy Blume said, "Yes, rejection and criticism hurt. Get used to it."

If you're overly sensitive to the opinions of others, it's time to start thinking more rationally. Remember: you can't please everybody. Sure, there are a few people you should seek to please, starting with your family (and, to a lesser extent, the people who sign your paycheck). But do yourself a favor and understand that trying to please everyone is impossible. Sometimes you just have to shrug and walk away.

Just pray for a tough hide and a tender heart.
Ruth Bell Graham

The Sacred Trust

> *Regarding life together and getting along*
> *with each other, you don't need me to*
> *tell you what to do. You're God-taught*
> *in these matters. Just love one another!*
> 1 Thessalonians 4:9 MSG

Loyalty is the glue that holds relationships, marriages, and societies together. When we make loyalty the hallmark of our dealings with others, we reap lasting rewards. But when we forget a friend or betray a trust, we invite consequences that are both troubling and predictable.

We live in a world that seems to be paying less and less attention to the ties that bind. Ours is a highly mobile society: we move from job to job, from relationship to relationship, and from town to town. But loyalty has not gone out of style, and it never will.

The Roman statesman Cicero observed, "Nothing is more noble, nothing more venerable than fidelity. Faithfulness and truth are the most sacred endowments of the human mind." Loyalty is a sacred trust.

> *The best proof of love is trust.*
> Joyce Brothers

This Is God's Day

Let all who take refuge in You rejoice.
Psalm 5:11 HCSB

Most of us have far more blessings than we can count, but sometimes, instead of trying to count them, we lose sight of them altogether. We're not intentionally ungrateful; we're simply overworked, overstressed, and overobligated. Nonetheless, we should pause at short intervals throughout each day to offer prayers of thanks for our blessings.

May we always give thanks to God for His blessings, and may we always demonstrate our gratitude by sharing our gifts with others. Let's celebrate this day and the One who created it. And may we invite our family and friends to join in the celebration.

A joyful heart is like a sunshine of God's love,
the hope of eternal happiness, a burning flame of God.
And if we pray, we will become that sunshine of
God's love—in our own home, the place
where we live, and in the world at large.
Mother Teresa

A Steady Purpose

There is one thing I always do. Forgetting the past and straining toward what is ahead, I keep trying to reach the goal and get the prize for which God called me.
Philippians 3:13–14 NCV

In 1797 Mary Wollstonecraft Godwin was born in London. She was the daughter of radical philosopher William Godwin and feminist Mary Wollstonecraft. At age nineteen Mary Godwin married the noted English poet Percy Bysshe Shelley. Later she authored the Gothic novel *Frankenstein*.

Mary Wollstonecraft Shelley once observed, "Nothing contributes so much to soothing the mind as a steady purpose—a point on which the soul may fix its intellectual eye."

Today is a wonderful day to contemplate the overriding purpose that guides your life and soothes your soul. What are you passionate about? What were you born to do? Find out and begin it today.

It is not a matter of thinking a great deal
but of loving a great deal,
so do whatever arouses you most to love.
Saint Teresa of Avila

The Power of Optimism

My lips will shout for joy when I sing praise to You.
Psalm 71:23 HCSB

Your thoughts are the things that determine the direction of your day and your life. How will you direct your thoughts today? Will you focus on your fears and your disappointments, or will you focus on the innumerable blessings that God, in His wisdom, has seen fit to bestow upon you?

God created you in His own image, and He wants you to experience joy and abundance. To that end He has given you a wide array of talents and opportunities. It's up to you to cultivate those talents and seize those opportunities—and optimistic thoughts will help you do so.

Today and every day celebrate the life God has given you. Think optimistically about yourself and your future. Give thanks to the one who has given you everything, and trust in your heart that He wants to give you much more.

The things we think are the things that feed our souls.
If we think on pure and lovely things,
we shall grow pure and lovely like them;
and the converse is equally true.
Hannah Whitall Smith

The Source of Our Comfort

May Your faithful love comfort me, as You promised.
Psalm 119:76 HCSB

We live in a world that is, at times, a frightening place. We live in a world that is, at times, a discouraging place. We live in a world where life-changing losses can be so painful and so profound that it seems we will never get over them. But with God's help, and with the help of encouraging family members and friends, we can recover.

During the darker days of life, we are wise to remember that God is with us always and that He offers us comfort, assurance, and peace. Our task, of course, is to accept these gifts.

When we trust in God's promises, the world becomes a less frightening place. With God's comfort and His love in our hearts, we can tackle our problems with courage, determination, and faith.

Sometimes the very essence of faith is trusting God
in the midst of things He knows good
and well we cannot comprehend.
Beth Moore

The Morning Watch

He awakens Me morning by morning,
He awakens My ear to hear as the learned.
The Lord GOD has opened My ear.
Isaiah 50:4–5 NKJV

Each day has 1,440 minutes. Do you value your relationship with God enough to spend a few of those minutes with Him? He wants to spend them with you.

As you consider your plans for the day ahead, organize your life around this simple principle: God first. When you place your Creator where He belongs—at the very center of your day and of your life—the rest of your priorities will fall into place.

Each new day is a gift from God, and if you're wise, you'll spend a few quiet moments each morning thanking the Giver. It's the best way to start the day.

Think of this—we may live together
with Him here and now, a daily walking
with Him who loved us and gave Himself for us.
Elisabeth Elliot

December 23

Doubt and Belief

Lord, I believe; help my unbelief!
Mark 9:24 NKJV

If you've never had any doubts about your faith, then you can stop reading this page right now and skip to the next. But if you've ever been plagued by doubts about your faith or about God, keep reading. Even some of the most faithful women are sometimes beset by occasional bouts of discouragement and doubt. But even if you feel far removed from God, God is never far removed from you. He's always with you, always willing to calm the storms of life.

When you're plagued by doubts, that's precisely the moment you should seek God's presence by genuinely trying to establish a deeper, more meaningful relationship with Him. Ask Him to help you and reassure you in your areas of unbelief. Then rest assured that in time God will calm your fears, answer your prayers, and restore your confidence.

We must lay our questions, frustrations, anxieties, and impotence at the feet of God and wait for His answer. And then receiving it, we must live by faith.
Kay Arthur

The Power of Prayer

*I sought the LORD, and he heard me,
and delivered me from all my fears.*
Psalm 34:4 KJV

Prayer is a powerful tool for communicating with our Creator. It's an opportunity to commune with the Giver of all things good. Prayer helps us find strength for today and hope for the future. Yet because we are busy people living in a demanding world, we don't always take the time to carve out meaningful moments with God. And when we neglect our prayer lives, we rob ourselves of the power and the peace that flows from the loving heart of our Father in heaven.

Prayer has the power to change lives, including yours. So make a regular early morning appointment with the Creator and keep it. Then, as the day unfolds, continue your conversation with God. When you do, you'll sense His peace, you'll gain His perspective, and you'll receive His power.

There will be no power in our lives apart from prayer.
Angela Thomas

When to Improve the World

*A good person produces good deeds
and words season after season.*
Matthew 12:35 MSG

During the dark days of World War II, Anne Frank and her family, along with four other people, spent twenty-five months in a hidden annex of rooms above Anne's father's office in Amsterdam. Eventually, the Franks and their friends were discovered by German authorities and deported to Nazi concentration camps. Nine months later Anne died of typhus in the notorious Bergen-Belsen camp, at the age of fifteen. Her diary—saved during the war by one of her family's helpers and published in 1947—quickly became a classic.

Anne Frank wrote, "How wonderful it is that nobody need wait a single moment before starting to improve the world." Her words were true then, and they're true now: the best moment to begin improving your world is the present moment.

*How do I love God? By doing beautifully the work
I have been given to do, by doing simply that which
God entrusted to me, in whatever form it may take.*
Mother Teresa

December 26

Faith That Works

*Look at the proud! They trust in themselves,
and their lives are crooked;
but the righteous will live by their faith.*
Habakkuk 2:4 NLT

Through every stage of your life, God stands by your side, ready to strengthen you and protect you—if you have faith in Him. When you place your faith, your trust, indeed your life in His hands, you'll be amazed at the marvelous things God can do with you and through you.

So make this promise to yourself and keep it: make certain your faith is a faith that works. How? You can strengthen your faith through praise, through worship, and through prayer. When you do these things, you'll learn to trust God's plans. With Him all things are possible, and He stands ready to open a world of possibilities to you. All you have to do is let Him.

*Faith does not concern itself
with the entire journey. One step is enough.*
Mrs. Charles E. Cowman

Discovering and Rediscovering Contentment

> *I have learned, in whatsoever state I am,*
> *therewith to be content.*
>
> Philippians 4:11 KJV

When we conduct ourselves in ways that are opposed to God's way, we rob ourselves of His peace. When we fall prey to the temptations and distractions of our irreverent age, we rob ourselves of God's blessings. When we become preoccupied with material possessions or personal status, we forfeit the contentment that is rightfully ours.

Where can we find the kind of contentment the apostle Paul described in Philippians 4:11? Is it a result of wealth or power or fame? Hardly. Genuine contentment is a gift from God to those who follow Him. It is a gift that must be discovered and rediscovered throughout life. And it's a gift we claim when we allow God to dwell at the center of our lives.

> *When you accept rather than fight your circumstances,*
> *even though you don't understand them,*
> *you open your heart's gate to God's*
> *love, peace, joy, and contentment.*
>
> Amy Carmichael

Dreaming Together

When dreams come true, there is life and joy.
Proverbs 13:12 NLT

A barber in Canonsburg, Pennsylvania, dreamed of being a singer. So at the urging of his wife, he closed his barbershop and began a career in music. Before he was finished, Perry Como had scored a string of hits, including such classics as "It's Impossible" and "Catch a Falling Star." He also hosted his own long-running TV show.

Looking back on his career, Como said, "When I started out, I was so discouraged I wanted to quit many times. The only reason I didn't was because of my wife, Roselle, who always stood by me."

The story of Roselle and Perry Como shows that dreaming can be a team sport. When two or more people dare to dream big dreams together, nothing is impossible.

Sometimes our dreams were so big
that it took two people to dream them.
Marie T. Freeman

Spreading Seeds of Generosity

*Remember: A stingy planter gets a stingy crop;
a lavish planter gets a lavish crop.*
2 Corinthians 9:6 MSG

God's gifts are beyond description, His blessings beyond comprehension. God has been incredibly generous with us, and He rightfully expects us to be generous with others. That's why the thread of generosity is woven into the very fabric of God's teachings.

In the Old Testament we are told that "the good person is generous and lends lavishly" (Psalm 112:5 MSG). And in the New Testament we're instructed, "Freely you have received, freely give" (Matthew 10:8 NKJV). These principles still apply today. As we establish priorities for our days and our lives, God wants us to give freely of our time, our possessions, and our love—just as He has given freely to us.

We can never fully repay God for His gifts, but we can share them with others. Share His gifts with someone today.

*To show great love for God and our neighbor,
we need not do great things. It is how much love we
put in the doing that makes our offering
something beautiful for God.*
Mother Teresa

Paying the Price

Idle hands make one poor,
but diligent hands bring riches.
Proverbs 10:4 HCSB

Beverly Sills first sang on the radio at the tender age of twelve. Thus began a career that helped introduce opera to millions of Americans. Beverly was not only a gifted performer, she was also a magnetic personality. But even a monumental talent like Beverly Sills had to work hard to be successful.

Author Paula Rinehart once pointed out, "God knows that the strength that comes from wrestling with our fears will give us wings to fly." So the next time you're tempted to cut corners, remember that shortcuts to success are few and far between—and not always wise. While you're waiting for the curtain to rise on your big performance, be patient, keep working, and be willing to pay the price. After all, where you're going is well worth it, even if it takes a little longer.

If I had given you any parting advice it would, I think,
all have been comprised in this one sentence:
to live up always to the best and highest you know.
Hannah Whitall Smith

God's Limitless Love for You

The LORD your God is God of gods and Lord of lords,
the great God, mighty and awesome.
Deuteronomy 10:17 NIV

Because God's power is limitless, it is far beyond the comprehension of mortal minds. Yet even though we cannot fully understand the heart of God, we can be open to His love.

God's ability to love is not constrained by temporal boundaries or by earthly limitations. The love that flows from the heart of God is infinite—and today presents yet another opportunity to celebrate that love.

You are a glorious creation, a unique individual, a beautiful example of God's handiwork. God's love for you is limitless. Accept that love, acknowledge it, and share it with others. You can make the world a better place just by being you.

The greatness of His power to create and design and
form and mold and make and build and arrange defies
the limits of our imagination. And since He created
everything, there is nothing beyond His power
to fix or mend or heal or restore.
Anne Graham Lotz

Notes

Notes

These pages have been provided for your personal journaling and meditation. _____

_____

_____

_____

_____

_____

_____

_____

_____

_____

_____

_____

_____

_____

_____

_____

_____

_____

Notes

Notes

Notes

Notes

Notes

Scripture References